Fast Second

Constantinos C. Markides
Paul A. Geroski

Fast Second

How Smart Companies Bypass
Radical Innovation to Enter
and Dominate New Markets

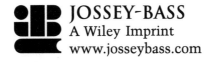

JOSSEY-BASS
A Wiley Imprint
www.josseybass.com

Published by Jossey-Bass
A Wiley Imprint
989 Market Street, San Francisco, CA 94103-1741   www.josseybass.com

Jossey-Bass books and products are available through most bookstores. To contact Jossey-Bass directly call our Customer Care Department within the U.S. at 800-956-7739, outside the U.S. at 317-572-3986 or fax 317-572-4002.

Jossey-Bass also publishes its books in a variety of electronic formats. Some content that appears in print may not be available in electronic books.

Library of Congress Cataloging-in-Publication Data
Markides, Constantinos.
  Fast second : how smart companies bypass radical innovation to enter and dominate new markets / Constantinos Markides, Paul A. Geroski.—1st ed.
    p. cm.
  Includes bibliographical references and index.
  ISBN 0-7879-7154-5 (alk. paper)
  1. New products—Management. 2. Technological innovations—Economic aspects.
I. Geroski, Paul. II. Title.
  HF5415.153.M338 2005
  658.5'75—dc22
                              2004010443

Printed in the United States of America
FIRST EDITION
HB Printing   10 9 8 7 6 5 4 3 2 1

Contents

Chapter One

Spotting the Real Innovators

Take this quick test: Which firm is the innovator that brought us online bookselling in the 1990s? If your answer is Amazon.com, you are wrong. The idea for online bookselling—and the first online bookstore—came from Charles Stack, an Ohio-based bookseller, in 1991. Computer Literacy bookstore, a successful retail chain, also registered an Internet domain name in 1991. Amazon did not enter this market until 1995.

Another quiz: Which innovator came up with the idea for online brokerage services? If you answered Charles Schwab or E-Trade, again you are wrong. Two Chicago brokerage firms—Howe Barnes Investments and Security APL Inc.—launched the first Internet-based stock trading service, a joint venture called Net Investor, in January 1995. Schwab did not launch its Web trading service until March 1996.

Both examples highlight a simple point that is at the heart of this book: the individuals or companies that *create* radically new markets are not necessarily the ones that *scale* them up into big mass markets. Indeed, the evidence shows that in the majority of cases, the early pioneers of radically new markets are almost never the ones that scale up and conquer those markets (see Table 1.1). For the last twenty years, the Xerox Corporation has been derided for its inability to successfully commercialize scores of new products and technologies, notably including the now ubiquitous personal computer OS interface developed at its PARC research center in Northern California. In reality, Xerox's failure is more the norm than the exception!

Table 1.1. Unsuccessful Pioneers of Radically New Technologies.

Pioneer	Technology	Year
Robert W. Thompson	Pneumatic tire	1845
Thomas Saint, Walter Hunt, and others	Sewing machine	1790–1851
Stanley brothers, Colonel Pope, and others	Automobile	1897–1905
Henry Mill, Xavier Projean, and others	Typewriter	1714–1878
Valdemar Poulsen	Magnetic tape recorder	1899
Alexander Parkes and Daniel Spill	Artificial plastics	1866–69
Juan de la Cierva	Helicopter	1930
John Baird and Francis Jenkins	Television	1924
Frank Whittle	Jet engine	1930
Transitron, Philco, and Germanium Products	Transistor	1952–55
Biologicals	DNA synthesizing machine	1981

Source: Francisco-Javier Olleros, "Emerging Industries and the Burnout of Pioneers," *Journal of Product Innovation Management*, March 1986, pp. 5–18. Reprinted with permission.

This may surprise people who have been brought up to believe in pioneering and first-mover advantages! However, there is no escaping the evidence. Henry Ford did not *create* the car market but the Ford company ended up capturing a lot of the value in that market in its first hundred years of existence; Procter & Gamble did not *create* the market for disposable diapers but it is P&G that ended up harvesting most of the value out of the mass market for disposable diapers that blossomed in the last fifty years; and General Electric did not *create* the CAT scanner market, yet it was GE that made most of the money out of this market. It turns out that when it comes to radical, new-to-the-world markets, the pioneers almost always lose out to latecomers.

This is a puzzle. The early pioneers tend to have the necessary technology and by definition enter the market much earlier than other firms. This should, in principle, give them first-mover advantages over any latecomer. Why then do they consistently lose out and surrender the markets that they create to other firms?

It's not because the pioneers are small or insignificant players with no resources or bad management. And it's not because their products are inferior to the products that latecomers introduce. Consider, for example, the market for personal digital assistants (PDAs). This market was created in 1993 when Apple Computers introduced its revolutionary handheld computer called Newton. Apple's CEO at the time, John Sculley, called it "nothing less than a revolution" and predicted that it would launch "the mother of all markets," with PDAs and similar gadgets constituting a trillion-dollar market.

Less than ten years later, PDA demand had grown into a billion-dollar market. While not as huge as predicted at the time of its creation, it had soared from zero to $1 billion in ten years and had established itself as one of the new markets of the Internet era. Yet even a casual observer of this market at the turn of the century could not fail to notice that the company that could legitimately claim to have been the creator of this market—Apple Computers—was nowhere to be seen. Instead, all the spoils from the growth of the PDA market had gone to firms—such as HP and Palm—that followed Apple into it. It is hard to see why. Nobody could claim that Apple lost out to Palm because of lack of resources or lack of expertise. Nor could the Apple Newton be considered an obviously inferior product to the Palm Pilot.

Why then did Palm succeed where Apple failed? More generally, why is it that the firms that create radical new markets are rarely the ones that scale them up into mass markets? And what does the answer to this question imply for firms that aspire to create the markets of the future? We aim to answer these questions in this book. It turns out that there are specific reasons why pioneers fail to scale up markets, and understanding these reasons will help you appreciate what the modern corporation needs to do if it wants to achieve radical innovation.

Radical Innovations

It should be obvious from the examples that we have used so far that *this book is concerned with one specific type of innovation*—namely, *radical* innovation. By this we mean something concrete. Innovations are considered radical if they meet two conditions: first, they introduce major new value propositions that disrupt existing consumer habits and behaviors (for example, what on earth did our ancestors do in the evenings without television!); second, the markets that they create undermine the competences and complementary assets on which existing competitors have built their success.

Everyone knows that there are different kinds of innovations with different competitive effects. It is, therefore, important to appreciate that what we say in this book does *not* apply to all kinds of innovations, just to the subset of innovations that can be classified as radical. Our interest is in radical innovations because these are the kind of innovations that give rise to new-to-the-world markets.

Not all innovations are radical. When we classify innovations along the dimensions of their effect on customer habits and behaviors and their effect on the established firms' competences and complementary assets, we get four types of innovations, as shown in Figure 1.1. The dividing points in the matrix are obviously subjective and our intention is not to defend the boundaries of a particular definition. Rather, our goal is to simply suggest that "innovation" can mean different things to different people, that different types of innovation exist, and that a given innovation may be more or less radical than another innovation.

Our interest in this book is on those innovations labeled as *radical* innovations in this matrix. These are innovations that have a

Figure 1.1. Different Types of Innovation.

	Enhances	Destroys
Major	Major innovation	Radical innovation
Minor	Incremental innovation	Strategic innovation

Effect of Innovation on Consumer Habits and Behaviors (vertical axis: Major / Minor)

Effect of Innovation on Established Firms' Competencies and Complementary Assets (horizontal axis: Enhances / Destroys)

disruptive effect on both customers and producers. They are based on a different set of scientific principles from the prevailing set, create radically new markets, demand new consumer behaviors and present major challenges to the existing competitors. The introduction of the car at the end of the nineteenth century is an example of radical innovation. *Incremental* innovations, on the other hand, merely extend the current proposition facing consumers. They introduce relatively minor changes to the product or service, build upon the competences and assets of the existing competitors, and tend to reinforce the dominance of the established players. The introduction of new features in a car (such as four-wheel drive, power steering, and fog lights) are examples of incremental innovations.

Major innovations are those that require fundamental changes in consumer behavior but build upon the established players' competences and complementary assets. For example, the introduction of picturephones could be considered a major innovation for phone manufacturers, as could the introduction of online banking for most banks. These are innovations that the established competitors will champion because they build upon their existing competences.

Often an innovation produces seemingly modest changes to the existing product but has quite dramatic consequences on competition. For example, the introduction of small cars (and small motorcycles, copiers, earth-moving equipment, radios, and cameras) by Japanese manufacturers in the 1970s brought havoc to U.S. manufacturers. The challenge was not so much technological as strategic—the new products required fundamentally different business models from the ones that U.S. producers were using to sell their existing products. This change undermined the established players' complementary assets and allowed the Japanese producers to steal market share. These innovations are called *strategic innovations*, and they are based on new business designs.[1] Examples of such innovations include low-cost point-to-point flying, online brokerage, and private label in fast-moving consumer goods.

Different innovations produce different kinds of markets. For example, Table 1.2 lists a number of markets that have been created through innovation—those on the left came about through radical innovation while those on the right came about through strategic innovation. Our real interest in this book is on the markets that are created through *radical innovation*—how and when they emerge and how firms ought to compete in these markets.

Academic researchers have been studying radical innovation for the last fifty years. As a result, we now know many things about the markets that get created by this kind of innovation. For example, we know how they get created and by whom. We know who colonizes them and who makes money out of them. We even know how they will evolve and how they will die. Our book builds upon this knowledge to offer advice to firms that aspire to create radical new markets. More specifically, our book addresses the question, How could big, established firms achieve radical innovation?

Table 1.2. New Markets Created Through Innovation.

New Markets Created Through Radical Innovation	New Markets Created Through Strategic Innovation
Television	Internet banking
Personal computers	Low-cost point-to-point flying
Personal digital assistants (PDAs)	Private label consumer goods
Cars	Screen-based electronic trading systems
Supercomputers	Generic drugs
Semiconductors	On-line distribution of groceries
Mobile phones	Catalog retailing
Video cassette recorders (VCRs)	Department stores
Medical diagnostic imaging	Steel minimills
Computer operating systems	On-line universities

Misconceptions About Markets Created by Radical Innovation

Over the past fifty years, a lot of ideas have been developed and much advice given to companies on how they can become more innovative so as to create entirely new markets. This advice has been hungrily consumed by corporations large and small. After all, what company does not want to become more innovative and what CEO does not dream about leading the way into virgin territories, discovering in the process exciting new markets?

Yet, as we will show in this book, this is nothing more than misplaced hope for the majority of big, established companies! There are two reasons why we say this: first, most big companies cannot create *radical* new markets; second, such companies should not want to *create* radical new markets.

Big companies are unlikely to create radical new markets for two main reasons. First, the innovation process that creates radically new markets cannot be easily replicated inside the modern corporation. As we will show in this book, radical innovations that give rise to entirely new markets are rarely driven by demand or customer needs. Rather, they are pushed onto the market by scientists working on independent projects all over the world. Supply-push innovation processes emerge in a wide variety of industries and share certain characteristics:

- They are developed in a haphazard way without a clear customer need driving them.
- They emerge out of the efforts of a large number of scientists and engineers working independently on seemingly unrelated research projects, who sometimes devise the technology for their own uses.
- They go through a long gestation process when nothing seems to happen until they suddenly explode onto the market.

Now ask yourself: Is this an innovation process that can be replicated in the R&D facility of a single firm? As we will show later, big companies cannot simply import or replicate such a process inside their R&D laboratories.

But there is a second reason why big companies cannot *create* radically new markets: they do not have the skills or mindsets for it! Even worse, all attempts to learn the necessary skills or adopt the necessary mindsets will not do the trick for them. This is because the skills and mindsets that they currently have (and need) to compete in their mature businesses conflict with those they would need for creation. Trying to incorporate the new skills and mindsets into the existing organizational DNA will end in failure.

This simple fact has not discouraged academics from continuing to offer advice to big companies on how they could adopt the skills and mindsets that will make them successful discoverers of new markets. For example, noting that big companies operate with so many rules and regulations that end up stifling creativity, several researchers have proposed that not only should the strategy process in the modern corporation be modified to allow everybody in the company to contribute strategic ideas but the culture of established corporations should be changed to encourage and promote activists and revolutionaries—rather than employees who simply obey the rules. Similarly, arguing that the incentives and planning processes within the established firm can suffocate the growth of new disruptive markets, other researchers have proposed a separate business-planning process to develop and nurture new business creation.

Yet, despite all this advice and good intentions, it is very rare to find a big company among the innovators that create radically new markets. Why not?

What people forget is that successful innovation is essentially a coupling process that requires the linking of two distinct activities: first the discovery of a new product or service idea and its initial testing in the market, a process that, if successful, creates a new market niche—an activity that we will call *colonizing* a new market; and second the transformation of the idea from a little niche into a mass market—an activity that we will call *consolidating* the market. It turns out that the skills, mindsets, and competencies needed for discovery and colonization are not only different from those needed for consolidation and commercialization, they also conflict with the latter set. This implies that the firms that are good at invention are unlikely to be good at commercialization and vice versa.

Some firms—primarily young, small, and agile—are good at colonization. Other firms—primarily older, established, and big—are good at consolidation. It's extremely hard, however, to find firms that are good at both colonization and consolidation. This suggests to us that instead of advising the established corporation how to adopt skills and mindsets that are alien to its DNA, we should be encouraging it to focus its attention on what it does best: consolidating new markets.

More Misconceptions

To reiterate, not only is the innovation process that creates new radical markets impossible to replicate inside a firm but—even worse—the skills and mindsets that big established companies have are not the ones needed for *creating* radical new markets. Nor can established firms easily adopt the skills of creation, because they conflict with their existing skills. This all sounds discouraging for established firms, but not everything is bad for them! They may not be good at creating radical new markets, but, truth be told, they don't need to.

That's because *creating* radical new markets is not where the money is. Real value comes from *consolidating* newly created markets, not from discovering them. And don't believe those that tell you that you need to be the discoverer of a new market to then consolidate it or that those that discover the new market are the ones that consolidate and conquer it. The evidence shows that colonization and consolidation are essentially different activities undertaken by different firms. The evidence also shows that if you have the skills to discover new markets, it's unlikely that you will have what it takes to scale up these markets; and vice versa.

As a result, the companies that end up capturing and dominating the new-to-the-world markets are almost never the ones that created these markets. Given this fact, why would any established company want to create a new market? Surely, the advice we should be giving established companies is how to scale up and consolidate new markets, not how to create them.

Not that the misconceptions about new markets stop there. There is now a widely held belief that even if a company does not actually create a new market, moving fast to colonize it pays off. The importance of pioneering or being first to move into a new market is something that generations of managers have been taught to accept as conventional wisdom. Yet pioneering the new-to-the world markets is simply bad advice for established firms! It's not that pioneering is bad in all cases—but for radical, new-to-the-world markets it is.

If we were to take a close look at how new markets get created and how they look in their early formative years, the pattern that repeats itself again and again is the following: the companies that grow to dominate these new markets are almost never the first into the new market. The success of the conquerors of new-to-the-world markets is based not on moving fast but on choosing the right time to move—and that is rarely first. In fact, the majority, if not all, of the pioneers of new markets rarely survive the consolidation of the market—most disappear, never to be heard of again.

The problem is that the pioneers of new-to-the-world markets die quickly and without first growing the market to a respectable size that would win them attention. As a result, they quickly vanish from people's memories and the glory that in truth belongs to them is thrust upon those who came after them and successfully scaled things up into a big mass market. Thus most people believe that Edison pioneered electric lighting or even that Gillette pioneered the safety razor. Yet nothing could be further from the truth!

As it turns out, the structural characteristics of radically new markets are such that pioneering by big companies rarely makes sense. Most established companies would do better if they follow the *fast-second* strategy. In other words, the companies that conquer radical, new-to-the-world markets do so by racing to be second.

What This Book Is All About

Our thesis is that it is impossible to offer proper advice on how to create or colonize new markets without first understanding where new markets come from, what they look like, and what it takes to succeed in them. It's only by starting our analysis with the question, What are the structural characteristics of newly created radical markets and what skills are needed to create and compete effectively in these new markets? that we would be able to identify the full list of skills and competences needed and the strategies that must be adopted if a firm is to be a successful colonizer.

It is important that we go beyond the generic question, How can the modern corporation become more innovative (and so create new markets)? This question assumes that the same prescriptions that will help a firm achieve product or process or strategic innovation will also help it achieve radical innovation. This is a fallacy. To appreciate the full extent of the challenge that established companies face if they are to compete effectively in young and immature markets, it is first necessary to understand how these markets get created and what they look like. In fact, the full extent of what established companies need to do or change to be successful creators of new markets is such a formidable challenge that many of them are better off not even trying.

The Structure of the Book

The next two chapters of the book describe in detail the early evolution of radical new-to-the-world markets. In Chapter Two, we discuss the drivers of radical innovation. We focus on demand and supply-side influences, arguing that, in the main, most radical new technologies are pushed onto the market from the supply side. The important implication of this is that new-to-the-world products that emerge out of these technologies are generally not well adapted to users' needs, a state of affairs that creates many opportunities for entrepreneurs to offer different adaptations or applications of the new technology to the market.

This in turn creates the conditions for entry into the new market, a subject we discuss in Chapter Three. We spend some time discussing why entry occurs on such a large scale, trying to identify where these entrants come from. For a variety of reasons that we examine rather carefully in this chapter, most markets cannot sustain the huge number of firms that enter early. Nor can the early market sustain the wide range of product variants made available by all the early entrants to the market. As a consequence, there is often a shakeout, both among different product variants and also among the firms that supply them. What emerges is a well-defined product—a sort of product standard, which we will refer to as a *dominant design*—that comes to define the market and gives it its particular shape. This in turn creates the basic ground on which the market subsequently evolves.

In the short run, the emergence of what we call a *dominant design* lays the groundwork for the rapid expansion of the market, bringing in a number of cohorts of different types of consumers who together make up the mass market. The chapter explores the process by which this occurs. In the longer run, the dominant design shapes the nature of competition that occurs in the market, and this in turn shapes its future evolution. The rest of the book explores the implications of these facts and figures of newly created markets.

Having described how radical new-to-the-world markets get created and what they look like in their early years, we then embark on an exploration of the managerial implications of our analysis. Looking at a new market from the perspective of an established company operating on the periphery of the new market, these are the issues that this established player faces:

- Should I be in the business of creating such radical markets myself or should I let others create them for me?
- If I do decide to enter a radical new market, when should I make my move?
- Once I enter the new market, how do I conquer it by scaling it up?
- Once I scale it up, how do I position myself in a market that has grown into a mass market?

We devote a chapter to each of these issues. Thus, in Chapter Four we examine what skills, attitudes, and processes are needed to be successful in market creation. We show that these skills and competencies are not only different from those that established companies have but also conflict with them. This implies that established firms are unlikely to be good at creating new markets. In our opinion, what the established corporation ought to focus on is not creating new markets but taking the markets that start-up firms have created and scaling them up into mass markets. This is the area where the established corporation has unique advantages over the small start-up firms and should therefore be the focal area of their attention. This strategy of open innovation will lead to a radical redesign of the organizational structure of the modern corporation, something that we see in other creative industries as well.

We pick up the issue of how to scale up new markets in Chapter Five. As a way of introducing the discussion of what is involved in scaling up, we revisit the "crossing of the chasm" problem: how to grow the initial niche into a mass market. Scaling up is really about expanding off an initial, modest penetration in the market, and it should follow naturally from whatever it is you are doing to establish a dominant design.

For a firm to establish its own product variant as the dominant design in the industry is of paramount importance. This requires several tactics and strategies:

- Getting prices down, usually by making the product "good enough" and investing in learning as well as in new plants to exploit scale economies
- Deciding whether the design is going to be open or proprietary
- Securing suppliers of complementary assets
- Winning the expectations game with consumers

Chapter Five explores how a company can do all this.

Given the burnout of early pioneers in new radical markets, one key question for any established firm is, When should I attempt to enter the new market? This is the subject matter of Chapter Six. Most established firms confronted with a new technological possibility either choose to close their eyes and ignore it or to rush right in before the opportunity disappears. In most cases, both these options are foolish. The best strategy for big, established firms to adopt is what we call the *fast-second* strategy. (In fact, the choice between being a colonizer or a consolidator is really a choice between being a first mover or a fast second mover.)

As an example of a fast-second strategy, consider the case of a firm in a very new market. A first-mover strategy would involve getting in there quickly and producing your own product variants;

a fast-second strategy would involve waiting for the dominant design to begin to emerge before moving. Meanwhile, a traditional second-mover strategy would involve waiting for the dominant design to be completely established and accepted in the market, and then producing a me-too product under that standard.

We all know what the second-mover strategy involves—competing on costs and low prices. The first-mover strategy is very attractive, but the odds of success are low (as we show in Chapter Three). That leaves the very interesting possibility of playing a fast-second strategy in such markets, a strategy that IBM made famous in mainframes (and one that others have followed successfully as well, such as GE in CT scanners, JVC in video recorders, Canon in cameras, Black & Decker in food processors, P&G in diapers, Sharp in fax machines, and Texas Instruments in pocket calculators).

Once the market is scaled up, the firm has to decide what strategic position to claim as its own in this market. You cannot sell everything to everybody. Since there are several viable positions in any industry, your task is to choose which one to claim as your own. This is what developing a well-differentiated strategy is all about. Chapter Seven explains how to make these strategic decisions.

Finally, Chapter Eight summarizes our analysis and offers our final thoughts on how established companies could position themselves to take advantage of the innovation possibilities of the twenty-first century. We argue that creative industries such as film or theater have a lot to offer in terms of ideas on how the modern corporation ought to be structured and how it should go about innovating. We also explore how a company can compete with dual strategies. An established firm that has successfully moved into and scaled up a new-to-the-world market is now operating in two kinds of markets: its old, mature market and the new market it has just colonized. The key success factors in the two markets are different and the competencies needed in each are also different. This is the problem that any diversifier faces, but the real complications arise if the competencies required to compete in the two markets are not only different but also in conflict with each other. How then can a firm manage two conflicting games? The chapter shows how this could be achieved either through separation or by becoming ambidextrous.

Chapter Two

Where Do Radical Innovations Come From?

Television, the Internet, cars, personal computers, beta blockers, PDAs, calculators, mobile phones, aspirin—the list of major innovations that have fundamentally transformed our lives and created new markets and new businesses in the process is seemingly endless. We only appreciate what they really have done for us when we try to recall the past or imagine a future without them. The longer they have been with us, and the more deeply ingrained they are in our lives, the harder this is. These major breakthroughs are what we call radical innovations, and they are interesting because they are what underlie the emergence of new-to-the-world markets.

In this chapter, we describe the process by which radical innovations come about and how they lead to the creation of new markets. The innovation process that leads to these kinds of markets is unique and cannot be easily replicated inside the R&D facility of an established firm, no matter how much time or resources are put into the effort. This has serious implications for the modern corporation, which we explore in the rest of the book.

These are the essential points of our argument:

- Radical innovations that create new-to-the-world markets are disruptive for both customers and producers.
- As a result, these kinds of innovations are rarely driven by demand or immediate customer needs. Instead, they result from a supply-push process that originates from those responsible for developing the new technology.

- Such innovations typically lack champions either in the form of lead consumers or of existing market leaders.

- Supply-push innovations share certain characteristics: they are developed in a haphazard manner without a clear customer need driving them; they emerge out of the efforts of a large number of scientists working independently on totally unrelated research projects, who devise the technology for their own uses; and they go through a long gestation process when nothing seems to happen—then they suddenly explode onto the market. This is an innovation process that cannot be easily replicated in the R&D facility of a single firm.

- These kinds of innovations initially create small niches on the periphery of well-established markets. This makes them unattractive to established firms.

Radical Innovations Are Disruptive

To understand how radical innovations come about, keep one thing in mind—these innovations are disruptive to both consumers and producers. They are disruptive to consumers because they introduce products and value propositions that change prevailing consumer habits and behaviors in a major way. They are disruptive to producers because the markets that they create undermine the competences and complementary assets on which existing competitors have built their success. Let's explore what this means.

Many innovations extend and develop existing activities, enabling us to continue to do what we are currently doing, only a bit better. These are called *incremental innovations*. For example, the laptop computer that this book is being written on is a lot lighter and faster than its predecessor of five years ago, which was itself a quantum improvement on the one that it displaced five years previously. Important and liberating as each of these changes are, none of them really rank in importance compared with the original introduction of a laptop computer to displace the desktop personal computer, which had in its turn displaced typewriters some years before.

Each new laptop enables us to do more of what we were doing before; no matter how big these increments are, each one taken in turn is clearly just an incremental improvement. However, the jump from typewriters to personal computers and then laptops represents a step change, one that has proved to be the source of a cascade of changes that has made a noticeable difference in how we live and work. The result of all these changes is that we have been able to switch from typing to word processing to browsing on the Internet (and many other things) and to do so on the move and not just at our desks. As a consequence, we now do some things quite differently from the way we once did them, and other things that we now do were never possible before.

The changes caused by such radical innovations have profound, often disruptive effects on both consumers and producers up and down existing value chains. Consumers faced with new goods and services based on radical innovations have to learn about these new products—not only what they are but how to use them and sometimes how to appreciate the benefits that they bring. Consumers must break habits, and change their purchasing and consumption patterns. Sometimes they must make costly investments in learning how to use the new product. Among other things, this can involve shouldering serious risks. (Will my investment in this new product be wasted? What will this new product do—if it actually works, that is?) Taken together, these various obstacles to change are sometimes called *switching costs* by economists, and it is a complete no-brainer to observe that the switching costs associated with adopting an innovation are almost always higher for radical than for incremental innovations.

Much the same applies to producers—the associated costs here are sometimes called *adjustment costs*. New radical innovations frequently follow the discovery or development of new technologies, and they often demand the development of new skills and new ways of doing business. These changes affect not only the producers of both the new and old products but also the many other firms that produce complementary goods or provide ancillary services. Such changes often reach upstream or downstream to transform supply chains, distribution channels, and delivery logistics. It is sometimes said that every product has its own infrastructure—its own particular value chain—and if that's the case, then it can be said that a new product based on a radical innovation would require the development of a whole new infrastructure. Therefore, as a new product displaces one or more established products, old infrastructures have to be destroyed and new ones built. Radical innovations also induce changes in the valuation of assets and skills and in patterns of behavior by producers, their suppliers, distributors, wholesalers, and retailers.

In short, radical innovations create new markets and destroy old ones. In a way, all this helps to explain why radical innovations are disruptive: they introduce big changes into our lives. No one likes change unless it is clear that it is for the better. But here lies the problem: for firms that have carefully built up businesses around existing products, new products are always a threat. They cannibalize existing activities and demand new (and sometimes rather risky) investments in doing new things (or doing old things in new ways). Radical innovations also challenge consumers and force them to reconsider their behavior in ways that may expose them to considerable risk.

What is more, the way that producers and consumers typically evaluate these risks often creates further problems. It is in the nature of radical innovations that the new products and services that they introduce are new and unfamiliar. It is, therefore, very difficult for anyone—producers and consumers alike—to assess just what the benefits are. The costs of change, however, are far more immediate and are usually much easier for everyone to assess. Hence, when really new products or services come to market, they come with promises that are hard to evaluate and threats that usually seem much easier to see and assess. Therefore, first reactions are not always positive. Under these circumstances, it is not at all obvious who would be seriously interested in championing a radical innovation.

This is an important point to appreciate because it raises a very interesting puzzle: since radical innovations require major changes from both consumers and producers and since the benefits of change are hard to assess early on, *neither consumers nor producers would have an incentive to champion radical new markets!* Who, then, introduces radical new innovations in our lives?

Radical Innovations Are Not Demand-Driven

Perhaps not surprisingly, radical innovations that give rise to entirely new markets are rarely driven by demand or customer needs. Demand-driven innovations can, at best, only account for incremental innovations that develop and extend existing markets. Such innovations usually come in the form of either product extensions or process innovations; valuable as they are, they cannot help us understand where new radical markets come from.

This statement may surprise readers, especially those with a marketing background. How could an innovation succeed if it is not based on some unmet customer demand? The answer is that for any innovation to succeed it must, indeed, meet a customer need in an economical way. However, the fact that a new product or service must meet some demand to be successful does *not* mean that it is demand that necessarily stimulated the development of that innovation! For example, there was and still is great demand for 3M's Post-it notes, but it's hard to argue that the discovery of this product came about because customers demanded it!

For a start, demand for a product or service might just as easily emerge *after* that product has been produced as before. How many nineteenth-century families went to bed praying for the development of television to entertain them on long rainy nights? How many of them planned to spend their Thursday evenings watching *Friends*? Indeed, how many consumers actually perceived the need for a Walkman or bubble gum or even music downloaded through the Internet before these products and services actually appeared in the market? Thinking through the list of radical innovations noted earlier, it seems likely that in every case people learned to love them after they were developed and put on the market, not before.

Furthermore, any theory that says that demand is the main driver of radical innovation stumbles on the fact that most attempts to produce new innovations result in failure. If demand existed for the new product, why did the product fail in the end? It is, therefore, hard to understand how demand can be a major driver of innovation—it may be important in determining which innovations succeed or fail on the market, but it cannot be the driving force behind the vast flood of unwanted or undervalued innovations produced by hopeful entrepreneurs.

This is not to deny the fact that users and consumers do sometimes play a lead role in stimulating innovation, but such situations are rather rare. Some of the best-known examples of user-led innovation emerge from public sector purchasing (that is, the government). For example, the development of the computer owed more than a little to the activities of purchasers like the U.S. Census Bureau and Defense Department. Much the same could be said about the development of the semiconductor industry. Other famous examples of user-led innovations include the role played by airlines like Pan Am in the development of the Boeing 747 and the activities of car makers around the world in stimulating their suppliers to produce new lightweight materials, stronger adhesives, and even robots. In fact, user-led innovation processes are often a feature of innovative activity in the engineering sector.[1]

However, these user-led innovations are the exceptions rather than the rule. In fact, demand is a more important stimulant of incremental than of radical innovation. Incremental innovations are based on extending and developing existing activities. Consumers are likely to be familiar with well-established products and to understand enough about them to at least outline priorities for further development. Furthermore, since a market already exists for the product, consumers will have relatively little trouble in communicating these priorities to producers, who in turn will be as anxious to satisfy them as the competition in the market can make them. Radical innovations are, however, a different story. The scale of change involved is much larger, and this creates a resistance that affects both consumers and producers. All this does not mean that users play no role whatsoever in bringing out radical innovations, just that they are unlikely to be the main drivers.

For example, the development of the Internet could hardly be described as a demand-driven innovation, despite some appearances to the contrary. True, the first computer networks were financed by a potential user—a unit of the U.S. Department of Defense called DARPA (the Defense Advanced Research Projects Agency). However, this agency had a blue-sky brief; its people were not so much looking for specific things as they were thinking about general sorts of problems. One of these was to design communications networks that would be less vulnerable in time of war. Another was to improve the interaction between a computer and its users, if only to help ensure that the computer (in those days, it was a room-sized mainframe) was fully utilized.

The first network that appeared on the market—christened ARPANET—served to connect about a half a dozen institutions and was designed mainly to see if it could be done. Having managed to establish the network, the various users (typically, computer scientists in university research labs) found plenty of ways to put it to use (not all of them work-related). This is the point at which demand began to kick in seriously. ARPANET initially connected three universities, a consulting firm, and a research institute, but by the mid-1980s more than a thousand host computers were connected, a number that passed the million mark early in the 1990s. As the network grew, software protocols (such as TCP/IP, HTML, and HTTP) needed to be established to enable all these computers to talk to each other, and as less and less sophisticated users began to use the network, demand grew for simpler operating systems that would enable people without Ph.D.'s in a dozen computing languages to navigate in the new world. The big event that opened up the World Wide Web to ordinary users was, of course, the Netscape browser. As users got more and more comfortable with using the Internet, their role in guiding its subsequent development grew. However, almost none of these users were present at the very beginning when the Internet first began to take shape, and that is the point.

Radical Innovations Are Supply-Pushed to the Market

If users are not the major driver of most of the radical innovations that create new markets, then these innovations must somehow be pushed onto the market by forces on the supply side. It is important to get a sense of how this occurs.

An Example: The TV Market

Consider, for example, the creation of the market for television. Arguably, its ultimate founder was one Joseph May. He was an engineer who, while doing routine maintenance operations on a trans-Atlantic undersea telegraph cable in 1872, noticed that the ability of a material called selenium to conduct electricity was affected by light. Photosensitivity like this makes it possible to use selenium to measure the intensity of light and to translate variations in coloring or shading in a picture into a pulsating electrical current.

Within a decade of May's fortuitous discovery, a leading learned journal had proclaimed, *"The complete means of seeing by telegraphy has been known for some time by scientific men."* However, it took several further decades to make the step from this level of scientific understanding to the kind of broadcast television that keeps so many people glued to the screen for thirty hours a week. Although much of the technical work was done by obsessive, single-minded scientists and engineers like Philo Farnsworth and John Logie Baird, the great champion of television turned out to be the legendary head of RCA, David Sarnoff. He was a visionary whose interest in television was at least partly spurred by his fear of what it might do to RCA's commanding position in radio.

Notice that so far in the development of this new product, consumers have not even appeared as a driving force. On the other hand, one would not want to say that television came about wholly by accident. May's discovery was accidental, but Farnsworth, Baird, and Sarnoff all knew what they were doing. What seems to have happened is that somehow, someone stumbled across an advance in knowledge that seemed likely to yield a new product. At this very early stage of recognition, the new product can hardly be described as anything more than a possibility—moving it forward might or might not result in something useful.

Anyone who has watched pharmaceutical firms screen for new chemical entities will recognize just what we are talking about here: the advance in knowledge yields no more than a set of possibilities that, after serious and systematic study, might just result in something useful. The fact that a medicine that initially looked like something that might help heart patients eventually developed into a miracle cure for erectile dysfunction is an equally familiar story—indeed, some say that it is part of the charm of the whole process that the outcomes often seem wholly unrelated to what people thought they would find when the process started.

Supply-Driven Innovations

This kind of innovation process has a name—*supply push*—and it is one that appears in a very wide variety of industries. Supply-push innovation processes are difficult to understand because they emerge in the absence of a clear demand driver, a fact that makes many of the innovations produced by these processes look like accidents. When one reads stories like the development of television (or Post-it notes or Viagra or Aspartame or countless other inventions), one finds it very easy to think that new technologies typically emerge in a serendipitous fashion. This feeling becomes all the more powerful when one watches scientists and engineers at work and sees just how often they fail to fully appreciate the significance of what they are doing and how often the breakthroughs that they achieve are propelled by what seems like no more than inspired guesswork at best or just plain good luck.

However, appearances can be deceptive. The truth of the matter is that supply-push innovations often follow an ordered pattern that economists call a *technological trajectory*. In essence this means that scientists around the world working on a particular topic or area share certain beliefs and assumptions or paradigms. These paradigms set priorities, identify what the important problems are, establish acceptable methods for pursuing them, and condition expectations about what to expect from applying these methods to those priorities. This mental model, this sense of what one should do and what will happen if one does it, provides a guiding hand on the design and conduct of research projects that removes at least some of the serendipity from the whole process. While it is not always the case that one finds what one is looking for, it is rarely the case that one sees what one is not looking for.

The organizing power of paradigms goes well beyond their effects on particular research projects: paradigms organize the work of whole communities of scientists and engineers, not just isolated individuals. They help to define a pattern of common knowledge, goals, methods, and expectations that give a wide range of scientists and engineers in a particular field what seems like a common purpose. Paradigms create communities with shared values and expectations and for this reason they align the efforts of a wide range of otherwise independent scientists and engineers. Wherever they are and whatever they are doing, those scientists and engineers who share the same paradigm are likely to end up, in effect, fishing in pretty much the same way in pretty much the same pond. In these circumstances, it would not be surprising if the fish that different scientists catch in that pond belonged to the same species or at least to the same family.

One good example of a technology paradigm emerged from the development of streptomycin in the early 1940s. This discovery not only generated a new "wonder drug" following in the wake of penicillin but also profoundly affected commercial and research methods in pharmaceuticals. The inventor, Selman Waksman, licensed his patents to numerous producers at very modest royalties, triggering intense price competition in the market that benefited no one except, of course, consumers. As a result, patenting became an integral part of the research strategy of most pharmaceutical firms. Even more fundamentally, his screening methods—involving synthesizing and testing a great many organic molecules—came to dominate research methodology in the sector for many years.

Similarly, miniaturization was a major focus of attention in the development of semiconductor devices in the U.S. in the late 1950s, largely as the result of a push by the military. Although integrated circuits did not directly emerge from the research programs initiated by the U.S. Department of Defense, the military was quick to seize on the potential of miniaturization and together with a gradually growing private sector of users stimulated its further development. One way or another, the drive to miniaturization defined a research agenda—and a resulting trajectory of performance improvement—through a long series of devices that were ever smaller and more powerful. This agenda determined how people thought about what the important challenges were in semiconductor research, established priorities among competing research projects, and shaped the way that people evaluated the outcomes of those projects.

The organized research program that scientists and engineers follow means that there may actually be a pattern to innovative activity over time (possibly more evident with the benefit of hindsight than with foresight, and possibly more by accident than deliberate design). When a number of scientists and engineers share a technological paradigm, the result of their individual efforts is likely to appear to have been coordinated: one innovation rapidly leads to the next innovation, one application of a new principle may be followed by a series of further applications of that same basic principle.

The pursuit of these possibilities leads people to go shooting off in all directions. Some of these possibilities will lead to more breakthroughs and create more possibilities, while others lead nowhere. As time passes, the choices that people have made will lead the technology to develop in certain directions, and the fact that each breakthrough creates possibilities for further breakthroughs (and the knowledge and expertise to create them) will give that evolution a cumulative, path-dependent flavor. A process in which each possibility explored leads to the creation of more possibilities will lead to something that looks like a tree whose dense lattice of branches is built up around trunks and main limbs.

This basic branching process suggests that these inventions might come in clusters of related breakthroughs. Thus the original breakthrough in understanding the structure of atoms at the beginning of the century led to major trajectories in particle physics, cosmology, and chemistry. As scientific and engineering knowledge in each of these areas progressed, further lines of research opened up: the atom was split, the structure of DNA was revealed, and so on. Each new area of research has produced a rash of related discoveries, often by different, noninteracting individuals who share only the knowledge of the common branch and its main trajectory.

This discussion might sound too theoretical, but a recent report by the U.S. National Research Council (examining how the key technologies that gave rise to numerous new markets in the last ten years were discovered) demonstrates that what we have described here is in fact close to reality.[2] We reproduce one of the key findings of this report in Figure 2.1. Note how long it took for the technologies to develop and be commercialized, how scientists from government, universities, and corporate R&D facilities contributed to the development of the technologies, and, most of all, how the companies that ended up dominating the markets that developed were not even contributors to the key research!

The idea that technologies get discovered along a technological trajectory stimulates a further thought: as the inventions that emerge from different branches are applied in different sectors, their

Figure 2.1. Where Key Technologies Come From.

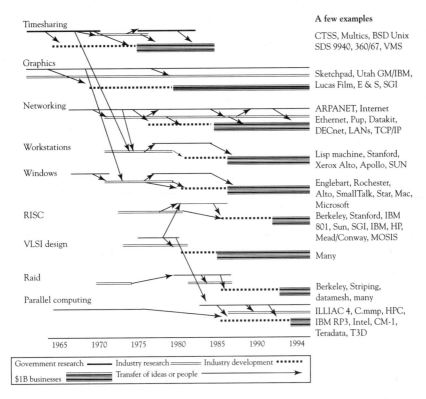

Source: Reprinted with permission from *Funding a Revolution: Government Support for Computing Research*, copyright © 1999 by the National Academy of Sciences, courtesy of the National Academy Press, Washington, D.C.

common technological base creates the impression that these sectors are somehow converging. For example, the gradually increasing understanding—and use—of digital technologies has now generated a cascade of innovations in computing and telecommunications whose uses have spilled over into the production of entertainment.

To summarize: new technologies often develop along technological trajectories independently of demand. The emergence and early development of a trajectory may look like an accident, but once the basic highway that the trajectory is going to follow becomes clear, progress along it is likely to be pretty much self-sustaining, following its own logic at a speed determined primarily by the nature of how scientists and engineers work. From any particular trajectory, all kinds of possibilities arise, all kinds of applications are possible, and so all kinds of new products and services are likely to emerge. The result is that many new innovations that are spun off from any particular trajectory are likely to appear to have been pushed on to the market by the scientists and engineers who have been working along that trajectory.

New trajectories are associated with radical breakthroughs in scientific and engineering knowledge and these are—almost by definition—likely to be a surprise or appear to be accidental. Such breakthroughs are likely to lead almost anywhere—or so it certainly seems to the pioneering scientists and engineers associated with the breakthrough at the time. And, it is these new trajectories that form the basis of many radical innovations.

The Role of Demand in a Supply-Push World

To say that supply push is a major driver of innovation does not mean that demand is irrelevant or that it plays no important role in the radical innovation process. In fact, the forces of demand play three important roles in the development of new radical innovations.

First, demand sets broad priorities for research. As anyone who has watched the response to AIDS knows, there are situations when potential consumers are able to articulate a need in a form that is clear enough to give scientists and engineers a fairly precise target to aim at. The clearer the expression of needs and the more able they are to finance the development of a new innovation that meets their expressed needs, the more buyers can contribute to the design and production process.

Second, demand is often important in determining when new innovations are brought to market. There is evidence to suggest that innovations tend to be introduced during cyclical upswings, when demand is expanding and markets both widen and deepen. Furthermore, the introduction of certain innovations is often timed with the arrival of new users on the market—they are introduced when they are ready for it, and not before.

The third and most important role for demand in the innovation process is that of selection. New radical innovations often come to market in a wide range of product variants, each championed by a different entrepreneur entrant. This proliferation is the way in which markets facilitate the exploration of new technologies and the matching of such capabilities with user needs. But at the end of the day, the only product variants that survive are those that meet user needs and the only way that anyone will know what these are is if users reveal their preferences by making choices. While it might well be true that demand is not the ultimate driving force behind most new radical innovations, it is certainly the case that no new innovations are successful until consumers have climbed onto the bandwagon.

Supply Push and the Emergence of New Markets

Supply-push innovation processes have one very important property, and this property has a profound impact on how new markets develop. Since the ultimate consumers of the new products or services that embody a new radical technology typically have very little knowledge of what the products have to offer them and how they would feel about them, the race to bring the fruits of the new technology to market is wide open. No one knows what consumers really want and no one knows just what exactly the new technology can do or how to economically produce whatever it is that results from the innovation. Anyone's guess is therefore as good as anyone else's, and since there are no real barriers to entry into the as-yet-underdeveloped new market, there will not, in principle, be any shortage of entrepreneurs willing to try out their own particular vision of what the new technology has to offer. Anyone who understands the new technology is, in principle, a potential entrant; anyone enthused by what the new technology might ultimately offer will, in practice, try to become an actual entrant.

This is basically what happens in all new markets created by radical innovation. Consider the television market once again, for example. Thirty firms were producing television sets in the United States in 1947, forty more entered the following year and another seventy-one entered between 1949 and 1953. The peak population of U.S. television producers was seventy-one in 1951, a number larger than the number of television set makers that currently operate globally and much larger than the current number of U.S.-owned television producers (which fell to zero after 1995). This massive wave of entry is a phenomenon that happens in the early days of all new radical markets. Since all entrants bring their own product variants to the market, the massive swelling in the population of producers is usually matched by a widening in the range of product variety that is wholly unmatched by anything that happens later on.

In point of fact, most new industries emerge from an uncertain cloud of unexplored possibilities that create something very much like a gold rush among would-be producers. This early competitive variety is unsustainable for a variety of reasons, and sooner or later a shakeout is bound to occur. Just what drives this process of consolidation is a matter for the next chapter.

Demand-Pull and Supply-Push Markets

Markets that originate from demand-pull pressures typically evolve very differently from those that emerge from a supply-push process.

Demand pull arises whenever buyers or users understand their needs and are willing to design something that meets these needs, find a supplier to produce it, and quite possibly finance the whole operation. Markets that emerge from this kind of innovation process inevitably reflect the actions of the user who kicked them off: the product that emerges is the one best designed to meet that specific set of needs, the first mover in the market is the supplier that user selected, and if anyone controls the market it is most likely to be the original user.

Supply-push innovation processes have quite different effects. When new innovations are pushed up by supply, they are very underdeveloped. The innovation is typically no more than a list of possibilities and it is anybody's guess as to what the right design is going to be. As noted earlier, there are no entry barriers; anyone who understands the technology can get in, and a great many do. To make any real progress in developing the market, consumers and producers are going to have to make a choice, to narrow down the wide variety of options that the supply-push innovation process has created. Just how that choice is made is crucial, for it determines which of these would-be producers is the winner, and what the product itself is going to look like.

Consider, for example, the personal computer market. The first personal computer for sale was, arguably, the Altair 8800, which was sold as a kit by mail order to hobbyists. In fact, these hobbyists had been making personal computers for years, largely for the fun of it and for their own uses. As they explored and developed the various component technologies, it gradually became clear that a whole class of potential users had no real interest in tinkering, and by the early 1980s more than thirty firms were making and selling personal computers (Apple, Tandy, Heathkit, Commodore, and others).

Some of these personal computers were better than others, some had good software and applications while others were nearly unusable—and those that were not bad were expensive. Even worse, very few of these machines could communicate with each other or use common software or common service facilities. All that changed with the arrival of the IBM personal computer, a product that established an industry standard and defined the industry. With that standard (what we call a *dominant design*), common software and a wide variety of applications emerged and prices began to tumble. It is hard to say that the personal computer industry came about as a result of IBM's actions—if things had gone IBM's way, we would still be using mainframes; on the other hand, it is clear that what we think of as a personal computer results from a vision that IBM did much to clarify and implement.

As noted earlier, all supply-push innovations share a peculiar property: since innovation leads demand, the target that inventors have to aim at is imprecise. Indeed, most new products are experience goods, and that means that the only way that consumers are able to form clear preferences about them is by using them. This is very important, and it carries three major implications:

- Since the new product does not meet an immediate, well-articulated need, it is likely to be a long time before consumers adopt it. Hence, one can expect take-up rates to be slow.

- Since there are no well-articulated needs, it is impossible to be sure exactly what the right design of a new product using the new technology ought to be. Hence, we expect the market to rapidly fill up with a wide range of product variants as entrepreneurs who sense an opportunity make a guess about what it is that consumers really want.

- Since consumer preferences will evolve with experience, there is likely to be as much post-innovation product development as there is before the introduction of the new product—or more. Hence, there are likely to be plenty of opportunities for a second mover to come into the market and win a place.

The upshot of all of this is that supply-push innovation processes are unlikely to produce a single new product or service. Rather, the nature of how supply-push innovations are developed means that they are likely to burst onto the market in a variety of forms. That is, when new technologies emerge, they are likely to do so in a confused and disorganized manner, in a flood of different product or service variants that embody different ideas about what consumers might really want and what might be possible to produce in an economic manner.

Supply-Push Innovations Create Niches

Radical innovations involve displacement: new products displace existing products just as the existing products once displaced other existing products when they first appeared. We normally think of new products in exactly these terms: cars displaced bicycles and carriages, personal computers displaced typewriters, and so on. In fact, when new products first appear they usually do so in what we regard as a niche in the market for the product that they are likely to displace. Actually, it is not even a niche. As we have seen, supply-push innovations generally produce a mess—a range of product varieties embodying different characteristics and imperfectly targeted at different users. From the outside this looks like a cluster of niches and we often remark that fragmentation is occurring. As the new technology gets explored more and more thoroughly and as the range of product variants shrinks down to a small number of core products (or dominant designs), these niches become better defined and easier to spot.

A niche is usually identified both by the product that it supports and by the way that product is produced. Tailor-made suits are a niche in the mass market for men's business clothes; luxury cars like a Rolls Royce are different inside and outside from mass market cars like the Ford Fiesta, and they are made differently and sold differently. Most markets have several niches and in many cases these niches are defined with reference to the mass market. We know that a Rolls Royce is a luxury car mainly because we all know what a Ford Fiesta is (and isn't). Equally, we all know that the main thing that identifies users of high-fashion designer clothes is that they are not users of the kind of clothes that the rest of us wear.

For a niche to become anything other than a niche, it needs to grow and develop. This means that it needs to attract a wide range of users. To make this happen, the new product has to appear relatively risk-free for potential consumers, prices usually need to fall, and someone must provide the wide range of complementary goods that these different users need (in Chapter Six, we refer to this as the *scaling up problem*). Above all, the new product must become established in consumers' minds, something that sociologists call *legitimation*. Consumers must understand the new product and accept that it can play a useful, if not essential, role in their lives. Legitimation processes often take the form of bandwagons, in which new users recruit more new users, who in turn recruit even more new users, and so on. It is easy to understand why this happens: after all, the most persuasive evidence about the usefulness of something is the personal testimony of someone who is already using it.

Thus new radical innovations are likely to make their first appearance in the niches of a well-established market. Most innovations that have the potential to become radical never realize that potential. They remain as niches in other markets or simply fail. Only a few supernovas expand beyond their initial niche—and those that do expand so much that they eventually displace the market they grew out of. Precisely how this happens is a subject that we take up in the next chapter.

Final Thoughts

The most important point to understand about radically new markets is that these kinds of markets are rarely created because of demand or customer needs. Instead, they get created in a haphazard manner when a new technology gets pushed onto the market. This simple fact has serious implications for the modern corporation, and it will take us until Chapter Four to unravel and explain what these implications are.

For supply-push markets, the initial competitive battlefield is as likely to be in a scientific laboratory as in any particular market; it is likely to take place among those who are more interested in the new technology than in the kinds of markets it may create, and most of the action is likely to be missed by those who are thinking about markets but know little about the new technology. When the new innovation emerges, it typically does so in a market niche somewhere. Most of the niches created by supply-push innovation processes either fail or stay forever as niches (and thus, in the eyes of their champions, fail). However, a few of these niches suddenly begin to grow rapidly and ultimately come to form a mass market of their own, one that displaces one or more previously well-established markets. To label them radical or disruptive is to acknowledge both the destruction that they create and the surprise that this destruction causes almost every sensible person on either side of the new market.

Chapter Three

From New Technologies
to New Markets

The supply-push process we have been discussing has one very strong implication, and it turns out to be the key for much of what follows. When science and technology push an innovation onto the market, the product or service that embodies the new idea is almost certain to be no more than a guess about what might appeal to consumers. Until producers understand exactly what the new technology can deliver and until consumers are able to understand just how to use the new product or service, there will be room for debate about just what that new product or service should look like and what it could—or should—do.

What is more, applying new scientific or technological principles to particular needs is not all that easy, particularly for complex new technologies that are not yet fully understood. Embodying these principles in a product or service that must be manufactured efficiently if it is ever to succeed in the market presents yet further challenges. Even when it is clear that demand for a new innovation exists and that it will form the basis of a large and profitable market, it still may well be unclear just how best to design and manufacture that product. And since there is no learning like learning by doing, it seems sensible to think that the right way forward for most innovators is to try out their pet idea and see if it flies.

This basic feature of supply-push innovation has important consequences for the way newly created radical markets evolve and what their structural characteristics are in their early formative years. Specifically, this is what we see happening in newly created radical markets:

- Despite enormous technological and product uncertainty, newly created markets are invaded by hordes of new entrants, *sometimes numbering in the hundreds*. Amazingly, this surge in firm population happens well before the new market starts growing. This is odd—one would have thought that entry would have been more attractive when the market is large and growing, not before.

- Not only is the new market flooded with hundreds of new entrants but product variety in the young market also surges to amazingly high levels. In fact, the rate of innovation at the start of its life is the highest that the market will ever see.

- Whatever it is that drives entry into young markets seems to create a surge or an almost uncontrollable cascade of entry. It is as if there were some kind of race that putative entrants were desperately struggling to get ahead in.

- Eventually, the wave of entry subsides and is in turn followed by what is sometimes a sharp, sudden, and very sizable shake-out that leads to the death of most of the early pioneers. The shakeout is associated with the emergence of a "dominant design" in the market, an event that signals the beginning of growth in the industry.

- All this takes a long time to play itself out. Thus the structure of new markets remains remarkably fluid throughout most of their early years and many more firms come and go than are left operating in the market when its structure finally settles down.

A Mad Entry Rush

One of the most surprising facts about newly created radical markets is that despite enormous technological and customer uncertainty and despite the relatively small size of these young markets, what we see in industry after industry is a mad rush by hundreds of firms to enter the new market.

Consider, for example, the car industry. Most of us date the beginning of the car industry with the arrival of the Model T in 1909. But the Model T was not Henry Ford's first car nor was the Ford Motor Company his first car company. Furthermore, Ford was neither the first nor the only producer of cars in the U.S. at the turn of the century. Though it is difficult to pinpoint the exact birthday of the car industry, the fact is that an enormous number of carmakers were operating in the United States before the Model T was introduced.

Indeed, more than *one thousand* firms populated the industry at one time or another! Fourteen firms entered the fledgling U.S. market between 1885 and 1898; nineteen entered in 1899, thirty-seven in 1900, twenty-seven in 1901, and then an average of about forty-eight new firms entered per year from 1902 until 1910. Thereafter, the surge subsided: from 1911 until 1921, an average of eleven new automobile producers started up per year, but that seems to have been it—very few firms entered the industry after the early 1920s until foreign-owned entrants started challenging the Big Three in the 1970s and 1980s.

This feature of the early evolution of car production is by no means unique to that industry. The market for *tires* followed much the same pattern as automobiles. From 1906 to 1911, an average of fifteen entrants entered this industry per year, a figure that doubled (on a per annum basis) between 1911 and 1922. Entry peaked at a staggering 115 new firms formed in the year 1922 alone, a year which saw the population of tire producers reach 274. As noted in Chapter Two, much the same kind of structural dynamics occurred in the television industry. Thirty firms were producing TV sets in 1947, forty more entered the following year and another seventy-one entered between 1949 and 1953.

Even more remarkable than the population of producers operating in the early years of the car business is the enormous variety in cars that they produced. In those early days, one could purchase cars powered by gasoline, electricity, and steam; cars with three and four wheels, and cars with open or closed bodies that came in a bewildering variety of different designs. Cars differed in their suspension, transmission, and brake systems and in a wide variety of extra or optional features. Not only was there a large variety of different types of cars on the market, most of the features that marked out the basis of this variety changed rapidly over time. For example, underneath the hood, a continuous stream of innovations led to the development of the four-cylinder engine by 1902, fuel-injection systems by 1910, electric starters by 1912, the V-8 engine by 1914, synchro-mesh transmission in 1929, and so on. In fact, the industry witnessed a wave of innovation between 1899 and 1905 that it never again experienced (although the periods 1912–15 and 1922–25 also saw noticeable waves of innovation). Furthermore, these innovations were introduced by a wide range of firms (the dominance of the innovation process by the Big Three occurred later on), and their use diffused rapidly throughout the industry.

Given our description of the characteristics of supply-push innovations that create these new markets, the reason for the entry rush and the amazing product variety in early markets should be clear: since supply-push innovation processes do not produce a single new product or service and do not result in new products that are ready to go to market from day one, the early phase of these markets is pure exploration. Would-be entrepreneurs exploit the technological and product uncertainty that pervades these markets by introducing a variety of products and business models, hoping that their product variant will win out by attracting the most customers. In a sense, they are doing nothing more than "trying their luck" to see if their pet product wins the race.

The early entrants to a new market share certain characteristics. They are enthusiasts. They understand the basic science and technology, and they are interested in pushing it as far as they can. They are willing to bet on seriously speculative projects that produce new products that are well beyond the frontier of current knowledge about that science and technology. They often assume that consumers share their enthusiasm for science and technology, and value performance in the same way that they do.

Since the basic science and technology is so new, no one is really sure where it is going. Each entrant is, of course, absolutely certain of being on the right course, but no independent or objective observer would place a bet in any direction. The enormous scope for different opinions about what the technology can do provides equal scope for many different types of new products, for many experiments with that technology. Each possibility is likely to have its own entrant, and each entrant is likely to have several attempts at developing the new technology into a new product. The result is market research in real time: a wild and turbulent phase of entry, innovation, and, for most of these early colonizers, exit. As everyone with a desktop personal computer and Internet connection knows, this is what is (still) happening in the area of e-commerce as of early 2004. No one is quite sure what the new Internet-based technologies—and the new businesses associated with them—are able to deliver, but there is no shortage of opinions and, as a consequence, no shortage of entrants willing to try their luck.

This early phase of market development is basically a learning process. On the supply side, firms are learning about the technology: what kinds of products it can support, how to produce those products economically, and so on. The more complex the new technology, the longer this process is likely to take and the more entry (on the one hand) and new product variety (on the other) we are likely to observe. Consumers also go down a learning curve during this early phase of industry evolution. They have to learn what the new product is used for and how best to use it. Different attribute configurations need to be examined, and evaluated. For some types of products, standards need to be set so that complementary products can be produced; for others, new products need to be legitimated, so that consumers come to regard them as something that they could—and possibly should—purchase.

All this suggests that the early structure of new markets is fluid in two quite different senses. On one hand, the number of firms entering the market is often very large, and firms come and go with great frequency. On the other hand, the structure of the products these firms offer is also very fluid: new products with new features also come and go with great frequency, generating many of the major product innovations that come to be associated with the market.

Two Additional Puzzles

The entry dynamics discussed thus far describe what seems like an avalanche of new entrants who arrive and try to colonize new markets. This entry is facilitated by the lack of entry and exit barriers and by the favorable technological opportunities available in young markets. This wave of entry is associated with a significant wave of innovation.

This still leaves us with two puzzles. First and foremost, the entry that we observe is a very large-scale invasion of a new market that seems to happen in a relatively short time. It is important to understand why things happen this way. Intuitively, it seems clear that this rush of entry is likely to involve more than just the leisurely exploration of a few technological possibilities by those innovators who are in the know. The pattern of entry in very young, radically new markets looks much more like a gold rush than a trip to an ATM: the number of entrants involved is large and successive cohorts of entrants follow closely on the heels of their predecessors, all in a relatively short time. Why this rush? This prompts a further question, namely: Where do all these entrants come from? Why is it that so many innovators seem to be in the know and are so keen to strive for a place in such a small and underdeveloped market?

First Puzzle: What Is the Rush?

The first question addresses the size of the entry wave that occurs early in the life of new radical markets and the speed with which it happens. The sense that the wave of entry which greets the birth of a new market is something like a speculative bubble is, of course, heightened by the shakeout of producers that seems to follow sooner or later—a bubble would not be a bubble if it did not eventually burst!

Three major forces are at work in the colonization of new radical markets. The first is something in the nature of an *information cascade*. Early movers into a new market enter because they believe it offers an opportunity to set up a profitable business and they are willing to shoulder the risks associated with being wrong about that opportunity. Other, more cautious would-be entrants will prefer to wait until it becomes clearer just what the opportunity is and just how profitable it will be. The important point is this: the very fact that early movers enter the market is informative for other would-be entrants, not least because it tells them that at least some entrepreneurs take a more sanguine view of market opportunities than they do. Needless to say, the more firms enter, the more likely it will seem to cautious would-be entrants that a genuinely profitable opportunity exists in the market and the more likely it is that they will bring forward their own plans to enter. This is classic herd behavior and it means that what starts as a trickle can easily turn into a self-sustaining flood.

Complementing this information cascade may be a wave of enthusiasm that fuels a tendency for all would-be entrants to overstate the prospects open to them in the new market. Enthusiasm is infectious, particularly when communicated by word of mouth. If the community of innovators or entrepreneurs who are the most likely potential entrants into a market is closed and tight-knit, then something like an *epidemic* might be created. Early enthusiasts become evangelists and mix with fellow community members creating converts who, in their turn, continue the evangelizing and convert other community members into activists or, at least, passive and uncritical supporters. Of course, each convert testifies to the truth or validity of the original proposition, meaning that the converted reinforce and re-enthuse the original early enthusiasts (and each other). Social dynamics of this type are easily able to elevate a conjecture or a bit of gossip into hard truth or indisputable fact in the minds of community members. The outcome is likely to be a bubble of enthusiasm, one that may actually exaggerate the appeal of the new market out of all proportion.

The second force that leads to the buildup of a wave of entry in the early phase of market evolution is the *provision of infrastructure*. Markets are surrounded by infrastructures that benefit all market participants. For example, the infrastructure for trading markets is a physical location, a set of trading rules, and a ready pool of traders; for manufacturing or service businesses, it is a mechanism that enables producers to meet buyers, a set of suppliers of specialized inputs, and a logistical system that ensures the delivery of the product or service to its ultimate users.

In many cases, new markets can be built on the infrastructure of existing markets—it is, for example, unlikely that Internet bookselling will require the development of new transport systems or that new soft drinks will necessitate the building of new types of supermarkets. However, new markets do sometimes require the development of new types of production skills or specialized inputs, and buyers almost always need educating about what the new product is and what it can do for them. Creating this part of a new market's infrastructure almost always requires expenditures by the earliest entrants if they are to produce or sell anything. However, once key suppliers begin to develop and buyers become alert to the existence of the new good, entry becomes much easier. If many would-be entrants plan to free-ride on the infrastructure-generating activities of the earliest entrants, then the creation of the new market's infrastructure by very early movers is likely to bring further entrants to the market in a hurry.

The third reason why a flood of entry often appears early in the development of a market is that many early entrants believe it is essential to get into the market in a hurry. They want to capture what are known colloquially as *first-mover advantages*, which arise whenever first movers are able to alter the conditions of the market in a way that disadvantages later entrants, who thus face higher barriers to entry than first movers did. (See Chapter Six.)

First-mover advantages are created when first movers are able to preempt entrants and monopolize supplies of scarce but crucial inputs (such as highly skilled and specialized labor, crucial raw materials, supermarket shelf space, and so on), or when they are able to lock in consumers and reduce the pool of potential buyers that later entrants draw upon to establish their business. If first-mover advantages exist and are important, then entrants will have an incentive to try to get to market first. The more entrants who appear early on, the more desperate potential entrants will be to get into the market before it is too late. The outcome is almost certain to be a rush to market that will look like a tidal wave.

An Example: The Internet Bubble. The recent colonization of the Internet has all the hallmarks of a speculative bubble (including the fact that it has burst). For a short spell at the end of the 1990s, virtually everyone with even the slightest entrepreneurial urge thought seriously about setting up a dot-com operation—and a great many people with more money than sense allowed themselves to be persuaded that they ought to be investing in this new dawn. Business schools, long accustomed to sending their graduates to work in consulting firms or financial institutions, found themselves scrambling to meet an apparently inexhaustible demand for e-commerce courses. And then, of course, it all ended in tears—the entry surge was suddenly reduced to a trickle and only a small number of e-businesses managed to establish themselves and operate profitably. It is hard now to look back at the Internet bubble and understand how and why so many people got it all so far out of perspective.

There were at least four drivers behind this flood of activity. First and foremost, the Internet offered a wide range of opportunities. Not only are there numerous things that one might try to sell on the Internet, there are also numerous ways in which it might be done. This exhausting list of possibilities creates more than enough space for many entrepreneurs to enter and find themselves a potentially differentiating edge. Second, many felt that with so many dot-com companies on the make, it was important to establish a brand name that might set the lucky owner of that name apart from the great unwashed horde. Amazon is a clear role model in this respect. Since it is a lot easier to establish a brand name and an associated reputation in a market that is sparsely populated than it is in one that is congested, the race to establish a name rapidly became a race to be first.

The frenzy that this sense of a race created fed into a third factor, namely the enormous publicity given to dot-com companies. No one who was awake during this period will have any trouble remembering the wave of enthusiasm created by all this entrepreneurial activity, nor will they have any difficulty in understanding how this wave of enthusiasm fed the surge in the number of dot-com companies that were formed at the time. As it turned out, however, the real race was for financial backing—to get to the financial markets with an IPO before investors lost their enthusiasm for e-businesses. The founders of early dot-coms were often able to float their companies for vast sums, and this had an amazing effect on the incentive to create—and try to float—new dot-com businesses. Whatever the logic that channeled vast quantities of equity and venture capital into companies that showed no signs of generating revenues, it was eventually exposed for what it was.

Second Puzzle: Where Do These Entrants Come From?

The second question requires us to try to identify the route that entrants take into new markets. It turns out that the answer to this question is straightforward: the wave of entry that acts as a vehicle for the new product variants that flood very young markets tends to be the work of a small, highly nonrandom sample of the full population of would-be entrepreneurs in the economy. Most of these entrants come from near the new market, guided by individuals who are familiar with the new technology and feel sanguine about its opportunities. Individuals in this nonrandomly selected group seem to appear on the market in a similarly nonrandom fashion.

There are basically three kinds of new entrants. First are the entrepreneurs who operate in the same or similar product markets in other geographical areas. Entrepreneurs operating in *horizontally* linked markets will certainly have enough basic understanding of the nature of the business to spot profitable opportunities as they arise, and they will certainly have the skills necessary to mount an entry attempt quickly and reasonably efficiently. Second are the entrepreneurs who operate in markets that are linked *vertically* to the particular market of interest. That is, individuals or companies who are either suppliers into or buyers from that market. Their operations in the market in question give them a privileged source of information and they have both an active interest in and at least some of the requisite skills to shape events in the particular market of interest.

Both these types of entrepreneurs are a source of potential entrants in all markets, new or established, and they are typically the major sources of entry into well-established markets. However, in newly created radical markets, horizontal linkages include established markets that the new market is likely to displace. Established firms that operate in markets likely to be displaced by the new technology face an interesting dilemma. They typically do not have an active interest in seeing the new market succeed. Indeed, they are often very interested in strangling it at birth because it will displace their existing profitable activities. They do, however, have an interest in being part of the new market if or when it becomes clear that displacement will occur. As a consequence, they constitute a pool of particularly able potential entrants but they may not be among the first entrants to arrive in the new market. We will talk more about this later in the chapter.

Third and finally, we have the entrepreneurs who know the new technology by virtue of working on *technological trajectories* close to the one that created the new market. This is a particularly important source of entrants for very new markets because, as noted, what drives the formation of many young markets is supply-push and not demand-pull factors. This means that the important signals of potentially profitable opportunities and the important skills needed to take advantage of them are to be found in a mastery of the technology that has enabled the market to come into being. Anyone familiar with the new technology is likely to be in a position to apply it in any particular circumstance (particularly if they partner with someone who has skills suited to the particular market being entered). Clearly, those would-be entrepreneurs who are working on branches of the trajectory closest to the new market are going to be more privileged than those who work on more distant branches.

The most immediate implication of this argument is that entry into any one particular new market is likely to come from a limited number of sectors. This is a pattern that is easy to discern in the history of most markets.

Examples: X-Rays, Television, Computers.

The first commercial X-ray equipment became available in 1896, shortly after Wilhelm Roentgen discovered X-rays in 1895 (passing them through his wife's hand and producing shadows of her bone structure on mineral salts). By the early twentieth century, electrocardiographs and encephalographs were introduced to the market and the technology was further refined through a series of minor innovations such as the development of better tubes, film, and monitors.

The early entrants into the business were a mixture of start-up firms and electrical goods firms. The real fun started in the 1950s with the development of nuclear medical imaging (1959), ultrasound (1963), CT scanners (1973), magnetic resonance imaging (1980), and digital radiography (1981). These were technologies that partially displaced earlier X-ray devices and enormously expanded their range of application. All these devices take pictures of the body but in different ways. X-rays, for example, record the absorption of short radiation waves by different parts of the body. By contrast, nuclear magnetic resonance imaging measures the gamma ray emissions of radioactive materials (which are first given to the patient), while ultrasound interprets the sonic echoes from different organs in the body.

By 1988, 320 entry attempts had been recorded into these new sectors by 240 different firms. In this industry, sales and entry went hand in hand as the new technologies introduced and developed by these firms expanded the market. Fifty-eight of these entrants were firms already established in the industry: seven of sixty-five entrants into the first sector, nuclear magnetic resonance imaging, were already established X-ray producers; eighteen of twenty-nine entrants into the last sector, digital radiography, were incumbent producers of X-ray machines or nuclear magnetic imagers or ultrasound machines or CT scanners or magnetic image resonators. The number of firms operating in more than one of these subfields rose from four in 1959 to thirty-four in 1981.

The interesting thing about the response of incumbents to the arrival of the new technologies is that they were typically slower to enter than start-up firms. It took fourteen years before the first incumbent entered nuclear magnetic resonance imaging (a wait that dropped to two years by the time that digital radiography was introduced). However, incumbents were often more able to survive in the new markets: the collective market share of new start-ups dropped steadily as these subfields developed. The first three start-up firms into the new nuclear magnetic resonance imaging subfield in 1954 had an average life of six years; by contrast, the first four established (elsewhere) players entered around 1967 and had average lives of nineteen years. Overall, thirteen of the first fifteen start-ups into these five subfields had exited by 1990, having survived on average for four years; only five of the first fifteen established firms to move into these markets had exited by 1990, and their average life was nine years.

Much the same tale could be told in many other cases. For example, roughly 180 U.S. firms had entered into the production of television receivers by 1989 (most left almost as soon as they arrived). Of these, about fifty had been producers of radio receivers. Leading the latter group was RCA; fourteen of the largest sixteen radio producers in 1940 entered into the production of television receivers. This group came to dominate the industry until the adoption of solid-state electronics in the late 1960s opened up the market to a set of Japanese firms whose mastery of this technology was more than a match for the remaining U.S. producers.

And the same story is easily discerned in the history of the computer industry. Three types of entrants initially colonized the production of mainframes: office equipment manufacturers (like IBM, Remington Rand, Burroughs, and NCR), whose business was directly threatened by the new product; electronics firms (like GE, Honeywell, RCA, and Siemens), whose mastery of the basic technology derived from operations in other industries; and new start-ups (like CDC, SDS, and Nixdorf) who arrived with the new technology (but never really had a major impact on the competitiveness of the market). The mini-computer market was colonized by firms from the scientific instruments industry (HP, Varian, Perkin-Elmers, Gould), existing mainframe producers (IBM and Honeywell), new start-ups with access to the new technology (like DEC, with its links to MIT, CCC, and Microdata) and, last but not least, spin-offs (like Data General, which spun off from DEC, and Prime Computer, which spun off from Honeywell).

Exit and Consolidation

Most of the new entrants do not last long. To take just one example, the U.S. automobile industry saw a very rapid increase in the number of producers, starting with the birth of the industry and continuing until about 1910, when the automaker population reached about 275. However, the surge of entry in the early years of the century led to a surge of exit by failed firms. In fact, most entry led to exit within a year or so. The industry never again hosted a population of car producers on anything like this scale.

Indeed, the next fifty to seventy-five years turned out to be a long and drawn-out consolidation (or shakeout) process. In the case of cars, *consolidation* meant two things. First and most clearly, the shakeout in the number of producers that occurred from about 1910 onward led to the emergence of the "Big Three"—Ford, GM, and Chrysler—whose collective share of the U.S. market rose from about 39 percent in 1910 to around 88 percent in 1968 (it has fallen steadily since then). Second and more interesting, the nature of the shakeout that occurred in the U.S. automobile industry led to marked regional concentration in activity. Detroit was not the original home of the car industry—the first Detroit producer was apparently Olds, who started up there only in 1901. Only 14 percent of the population of car producers operated in Detroit by 1905, but this rose to 50 percent or more in 1935. What turned out to be the key driver of Detroit's success is not so much that lots of firms opened operations there as that those who did tended to grow faster and survive much longer than those who operated elsewhere. Just why Detroit got so lucky seems to have been as much a matter of accident as anything else. What is clear, however, is that once Detroit became established as a center of car production, its dominance increased—and for better or for worse, its future was assured.

Dramatic as this story is, there is actually nothing particularly unusual in it. Much the same sort of evolution has been observed for a wide variety of industries ranging from beer, typewriters, rubber tires, and other relics of the so-called Old Economy to supercomputers, personal computers, computer operating systems, and many other New Economy industries. For example, from a peak of close to three hundred tire manufacturers in 1922, about fifty survived till the 1930s and only twenty-three were alive in 1970. And from a peak of eighty-nine TV manufacturers operating in 1951, numbers sagged to less than forty before the end of the 1950s. Color television production and the arrival of the Japanese producers in the 1960s completed the rout, leaving only a small handful of U.S.-owned producers at the end of the 1980s, and none after 1995.

The key features of the process are the same in all cases: the very early days of the new market see an initial rush of entry by vast numbers of producers and the emergence of a correspondingly wide range of product variants, each embodying the new technology in a new product or service with characteristics noticeably different from others already on the market. This wide range of producers and product variants displays an enormous churn year by year, with one year's new firms and new products displacing many of the new firms and products that appeared the year before. And then, at some point, a massive wave of consolidation occurs. The number of firms and product varieties fall, often very quickly at first and then gradually for long periods thereafter, and somehow, a particular product variant championed by one or a small number of firms emerges as "the product" and comes to define the market for that product. In the case of the car industry, the event that triggered the onset of consolidation was the arrival of the Model T.

The Emergence of a Dominant Design

What makes the Model T so special is that it defines what we all now understand as a car. As one traces back the early history of the car industry, the Model T seems to mark the time when something significant happened to the design and consequently the production of cars. Almost all cars designed and produced after the Model T are recognizable descendents of the Model T, while most of those that appeared before the Model T seem to be interesting and eccentric one-offs. A particular product design that identifies a market and defines the (narrow) class of product variants to appear in that market is often called a *dominant design*, and its emergence is a decisive event in the early evolution of markets.

A dominant design is basically a standard. It defines what a product is and what its core features are. It is, if you like, a platform, from which come a wide range of product variants that are distinguishable from each other without seeming to be fundamentally different. The core features of the product that are embedded in the platform determine what the product can do and effectively set parameters of performance that all variants built off the same platform share. This in turn means that the emergence of a dominant design sets performance standards and it is these that define the basic good and make it readily identifiable in consumers' minds. To be sure, different variants built off the same platform differ in their performance in various subtle ways but all product variants sharing the same platform will display performance standards that clearly differentiate them from apparently similar alternative goods built off different platforms.

The Model T effectively embodied a number of decisions about what a car was going to be, how it was going to be powered, how the power was going to be transmitted into motion, how the moving vehicle was going to be controlled, and so on. It is possible to produce countless different Model T cars that are observably different but share the same basic structure—they can have different colors, different upholstery, differently sized headlights, differently shaped tailfins, and so on. But whatever the color inside and outside, everyone knows roughly what these Model Ts are going to be capable of. Even more profoundly, once most consumers have opted to buy a Model T–like car, everyone now knows that they will require gas, tires, certain types of brake pads, service stations, roads, and so on. By contrast, if some cars were powered by gas and others by coal or by batteries, it would be much harder to organize the business of setting up refueling stations—and if some cars used rubber tires while others ran on padded wooden rims, the whole business of providing wheels for these vehicles would be much more complicated. However, once everyone has opted for a Model T–like car, then these problems fall away.

This is a fundamental point. A car is a lot less fun if it is impossible to buy gas easily or if it is hard to find replacement tires or a good and knowledgeable mechanic to fix it when it goes wrong. There is a real sense in which consumers do not buy cars so much as they buy transportation—a way to get from place to place—and this requires more than just owning a car. As every schoolchild knows, the period of massive expansion of car ownership in the United States just happens to have been almost exactly the same time when the U.S. government spent millions of dollars building highways all across the country. Thus the emergence of a dominant design stimulates investments in the infrastructure of the new product and at least for this reason alone, it is a major step in making the new product more attractive to consumers. When goods or services are consumed in combination, it is important to know how to bring them together and combine them. Since a dominant design is essentially a blueprint of the basic product, the emergence of such a design helps producers of complementary goods come up with products that can be fitted together with variants of the dominant design.

There is, however, a further reason why the emergence of a dominant design helps to stimulate the emergence of a mass market for the new product. Because a dominant design is basically a standard, it is possible to take advantage of economies of scale in production and to travel down learning curves. As a consequence, the emergence of a dominant design usually opens up the possibility of realizing massive cost savings in production, and this in turn means that prices are likely to fall. This was certainly the case with the Model T: thanks to Henry Ford's assembly line production methods, it was a steal at $850 when it first came out in 1909 compared to the alternatives on the market that cost thousands of dollars—and it sold for a cool $360 by 1916. At these prices, it is not hard to understand why it became so popular.

The emergence of a dominant design is important not only because it is a decisive step in establishing the new market but also because it triggers a severe consolidation in the market. Those pioneering firms that happened to bet on the winning design (or any firm lucky enough to jump into the market right when the dominant design is about to emerge) survive; all others die. The problem for most pioneers who rush into the market is that the arrival of the dominant design signals their death.

The champion whose product forms the basis of the dominant design often develops substantial and very long-lived first-mover advantages from being the product champion. *Notice, however, that most of these so-called first movers were not, in fact, the first into the market.* All of them were preceded by many entrepreneurial start-ups, now forgotten, whose work formed the foundation upon which these rather later entrants built. These "first movers" were first only in the sense that they were the first to champion the particular product variant that became the dominant design. They were first when the market emerged (not when the product emerged), and this, of course, is why they ended up with most of the profits.

It is important to emphasize three points from this: first, note that very few of the original entrants (that is, the pioneers) survive the consolidation of the market—most disappear, never to be heard of again; second, the consolidators who win in the end are almost never the first into the new market. Their success is based not on moving fast but on choosing the right time to move—and that is rarely first; and third, the things that consolidators do—such as entering at the right time, standardizing the product, cutting prices, scaling up production, creating distribution networks, segmenting the market, spending huge amounts of money on advertising and marketing—are exactly the kinds of things that create what we (somewhat inaccurately) call "first-mover advantages." By doing these things, consolidators create buyer loyalty, preempt control of scarce assets, go down the learning curve, create brands and reputation, and enjoy economy-of-scale benefits—all of which give them the advantage versus potential new entrants. Thus, even though pioneers are chronologically first into the market, consolidators are the real first movers—they are the first to the market that counts: the mass market!

How Does a Dominant Design Emerge?

It is one thing to understand why a dominant design emerges, and it is another altogether to understand how this happens. To understand this process, it is necessary to go right back to the new idea or scientific breakthrough that starts it all off. As we pointed out in Chapter Two, when a new idea emerges it is really no more than a list of possibilities. Since buyers generally do not have very clear preferences for things that they have never encountered or thought about before, it is not at all clear which of these possibilities makes sense. Further, since the science and technology are new, it is equally unclear which of these possibilities are likely to lend themselves to the kind of efficient, low-cost production that would result in a mass-market product. Anybody's guess is as good as anybody else's—and as noted, this is likely to stimulate a massive wave of entry and a proliferation of different product variants. In these early years, new product variants displace old ones, driving last year's entrants out of the market at the same time. The most notable feature of this phase of market development is the massive wave of entry; the second most notable feature is the churn in firms over time.

Stepping back, it seems clear that this is basically a market-learning process, a way to explore the new technology and test its limits. User-led innovation processes—those driven by buyers or users who know what they want—lead to lots of experimentation in laboratories. Supply-push innovation processes lead to much the same experimentation, but this occurs out in the open, on the market.

This happens in part because producers need to explore the new technology and find out what it can do. It also happens because buyers need to learn about the new products that the new technology brings. Buyers or users need to understand what the new product can do and how to fit it into their overall consumption program. They need to understand the different characteristics that are available and they need to value these. *Should the product be light, and, if so, how much is it worth to have a product that weighs a few pounds less? Should it have such and such a feature, and, if so, how much extra is it worth paying to get that feature?* Since the list of possibilities opened up by the new technology is bound to throw up a whole range of variants and a long list of characteristics that might feature on each variant, the task of sifting through these possibilities is likely to take some time.

Fortunately, the vast horde of would-be entrepreneurs who come into the market bring with them a wide range of product specifications, and the process of using and comparing their offerings enables consumers to accumulate quite a lot of valuable information in a relatively short time. Those product variants that are obviously inferior attract few sales and exit while those that seem to perform well for a wide range of buyers persist on the market until something else comes along that does the same job better.

Of course, all this experimentation and turnover cannot go on forever. At some point, the advantage of opting for a particular product variant becomes much greater than the gain from further learning, and it is in everyone's interest to choose the same basic design as a common platform for the market. That design becomes the dominant design on the market. This is an instance of something that economists call *network effects*—situations where everyone benefits if they make the same choice. This happens when consumers need to be connected to each other via a network (hence the name), but it also happens when the consumer or user base of a new product gets large enough to stimulate the production of complementary goods, or when it encourages producers to take advantage of economies of scale or learning curves.

Such collective choices are hard to make, if only because it is hard to coordinate choices across a vast number of people. There are, in principle, lots of ways in which it might happen: consumers might vote on which of the product variants they like best or some dictator might just choose a particular product variant on everyone's behalf. However, in market economies the choice is driven by the purchasing activities of consumers, whose actions are in turn affected by the actions of producers.

Basically, the most attractive design from the point of view of consumers is going to be the one that seems least risky (it works the way it is supposed to work), that offers the best support (it interconnects with more complementary goods), and is low-priced. Thus producers of different product variants need to assemble a coalition of buyers that is large enough to support the exploitation of economies of scale or learning curve advantages and large enough to stimulate the development of attractive complementary goods. To assemble this coalition, they need to find a product variant that works reasonably well for consumers with different needs. These actions often require major investments and therefore force firms to take large risks. We celebrate such actions by describing them as *bet the company* choices. Microsoft's choice to champion Windows (discussed later in this chapter) is one of the more recent and certainly one of the most spectacularly successful choices of this type.

In fact, the process by which all of this happens is very much like a bandwagon. A particular producer comes up with a product variant that attracts the notice of a good number of early consumers. This early consumer base attracts the attention of producers of complementary products whose efforts enhance the appeal of the new product. Further, early market growth justifies investments to exploit scale economies in the production of the new product. Falling product prices and the arrival of complementary products make this particular product variant even more attractive to even more people, justifying further investments in scale economies and complementary goods.

As more and more consumers join the bandwagon, word gets out. The experience early buyers have with the new product gets shared with more and more people, who come to learn about the product and how to use it. This in turn makes the product seem less risky and that too encourages more and more consumers to climb on the bandwagon. Once the process takes off, consumers not yet on the bandwagon created by the success of a particular product variant face a further problem: if they choose to buy something else, they run the real risk of being orphaned with a product variant that will attract little support and has no future. They will come to feel more comfortable making what is for them a second-best choice (but one that is the same as everyone else's, giving them the advantages of gaining access to network effects) than in making their first choice among product variants but being out there all on their own (without any network effects).

The Power of a Dominant Design

Windows, the computer operating system championed by Microsoft, is a good example of a dominant design. The cost structure of operating systems is particularly simple: they have production costs but no reproduction costs. That is, although writing an operating system incurs fixed costs, almost no costs are involved in producing more copies of that system. Furthermore, each operating system has a substantial learning curve that mostly consists of getting various bugs out of the system. Once the system is up and fully debugged, it costs essentially nothing to produce additional copies for sale. It follows, then, that the more people who choose to use the same operating system, the cheaper it will be for each of them.

In addition, very few people care about operating systems: what matters is applications. As it happens, applications have to be written specifically for each operating system. Hence, the choice of a dominant design for operating systems on personal computers matters a lot for applications writers. Once one particular operating system starts pulling out ahead of the rest, applications writers will have a strong incentive to write applications for it. The more applications that can be carried on the platform of a particular operating system, the more attractive that operating system will be and the further ahead of the others it will get. At this point, network effects begin to kick in. Since many people want to use their computers to share files and almost none of them want to learn how to use more than one operating system, it is in the interest of everyone to choose the same system. It is hardly surprising, therefore, that more than 90 percent of the personal computers powered by Intel chips use the Windows operating system.

Of course, it need not have happened this way. Windows was not the only operating system kicking around in the early days of the personal computer. In fact, MS-DOS was the early market leader and for a while OS/2, the operating system jointly developed by Microsoft and IBM, seemed likely to become established on the market. However, the release of Windows 3.0 in 1990 seems to have been the decisive event and the dominance of this operating system was established with the release of Windows 95 some years later.

It is easy to see just how important the establishment of Windows was. For a start, it created a near-monopoly because Microsoft managed to maintain a proprietary grip on the underlying software. Its command of the operating system market had even wider ramifications: it helped loosen IBM's grip on the personal computer market, it enabled Microsoft to move into a commanding position in the applications market, and it seems to have enabled it to come to dominate the market for browsers and perhaps other markets to come. Windows has also been good news for consumers. It is a system that almost everyone is willing to learn how to use, not least because they can use it on almost any machine anywhere to get access to all of their favorite applications. It has typically been available at a fairly low price and it is usually bundled in with new computers. Therefore, it has played no small role in helping to establish personal computers as a central feature of modern life.

Dominant Designs and Competition

Since dominant designs generally define a market, the competition between different putative designs that occurs early on in the development of a market is really a competition for the market. Firms that win this competition are unusually well placed to take control of the market that their winning design helps bring into being. They can use their early lead in the market to get down learning curves rapidly, and they can exploit scale economies to open up large cost advantages vis-à-vis later-entering rivals. They can integrate up or down the value chain to seize strategically important positions or gain control over key assets or inputs that rivals must have to compete effectively in the new market. Last but

by no means least, they have a real head start in building up relationships with consumers and in establishing a brand name. They
are, after all, the producer who created the market and this is a
reputation heritage open to no other, later-moving player. These
advantages are considerable and help explain why the Ford Motor
Company is still with us despite the fact that virtually all of its
contemporaries have long since disappeared.

These first-mover advantages are created almost naturally as a
by-product of the actions that pioneering firms take to help establish their product on the market as a dominant design. That is, they
arise when leaders take advantage of economies of scale to open up
cost advantages over later-arriving, smaller rivals; they arise when
early movers are able to gain access to key inputs that are scarce
(and deny later-arriving rivals access to them); and they arise when
early movers are able to lock in consumers by creating switching
costs that make it hard to buy later-arriving products. Such switching costs might arise from networks (later-arriving entrants may not
have created as large a network as the early mover), the reduction
of risk, or simply by the establishment of a valuable brand. One way
or the other, first-mover advantages are simply barriers that impede
the arrival of later-moving entrants into the market.

First-mover advantages are almost permanent competitive
advantages that early movers can realize and use to protect themselves against the competitive threats of later-moving, imitative
entrants. They come from being first to the mass market, but, as we
have just seen, this is not the same as being first in the market. The
numerous early movers in a new market are *colonizers*—they effectively explore the possibilities inherent in the new technology and
help establish what the new product is going to be, what it is going
to do, and how it is going to be produced. The one or two lucky
firms among them whose product comes to be the dominant design
are, effectively, *consolidators*. They are the ones whose actions create the market and set it on the path of becoming a mass market. It
is these consolidators who create the market and they are the ones
who enjoy first-mover advantages. First movement is not about

when you act so much as it is about what you do when you do get going—and very few of those firms who enjoy real first-mover advantages were chronologically first into the market.

Since a dominant design is attractive in part because it facilitates the exploitation of economies of scale and learning curve advantages, it seems clear that it is going to be accompanied by a major consolidation wave. Only so many firms can operate profitably in a market when economies of scale are large, and any first mover who is able to establish proprietary control over its design or seize control of key inputs is likely to make sure that very few of its rivals survive in the market. As a consequence, the structure of the market is likely to become rather skewed, with a small number of large firms competing among themselves and against a large number of very small players, many of whom operate in new niches created in the market.

Competition shifts from rival designs to rival variants of the same design. Firms differentiate their particular version of the core good from the same platform, giving rise to a much more limited range of variety on the market than before the dominant design emerged. Products are distinguishable from each other without seeming to be so very different. This makes it easier to compare them and makes it much easier for consumers to choose between them mainly on the basis of price. Most fundamentally of all, the emergence of a dominant design makes it much easier and much more attractive for new consumers to enter the market. It is, therefore, the event that transforms what originally appeared to be a niche market into a large, well-established mass market in its own right.

Final Thoughts

A market is a place where a good or service is traded. One way to think about it is to say that a market is basically a profitable business design—it is a production and distribution process that produces a product at a certain cost, and a set of consumers who are willing to buy the product at a price not too far above that cost.

At the base of such a business design is a product design. The product design that gains widespread acceptance among producers and consumers and comes to define the market is a dominant design. The process by which this happens is complex and hard to predict but it has many of the features of a bandwagon: early success tends to build on later success, if only because early consumers tend to convert others, spreading the good news by word of mouth. The dominant design typically emerges after a long period of experimentation and tends to persist for a long time thereafter.

The process features two major players: colonizers, who arrive very early in the market and help explore and develop the new innovation, and consolidators, whose championship of a dominant design establishes and grows the nascent market. Paradoxically enough, consolidators are the ones who typically enjoy first-mover advantages. More interesting, very few firms ever manage to act as both a colonizer and also a consolidator in the same market. This is the topic of Chapter Four.

Chapter Four

Colonists and Consolidators

It is one of the great myths of business history that the first movers in a new market end up dominating the market. Nothing could be further from the truth when it comes to new-to-the-world markets that are created by radical innovation. As we showed in Chapter Three, all such markets go through a predictable evolution: upon the creation of the market, there's a mad rush of entry by hundreds of new entrants to colonize the new market. Then, at some stage in the evolution of the market, a "dominant design" emerges. Upon its arrival, a dramatic shakeout and consolidation takes place: the hundreds of early movers that chose the wrong product design go bankrupt; a few lucky ones that happened to bet on the winning design survive, and a handful of these grow to market dominance.

The companies that survive the early shakeout of new markets are the ones that select or create the winning dominant product design in those markets. But even then, only a handful of these early winners will grow to dominate the new market. The eventual winners are the firms that proactively and strategically invest to grow the market and capture the mass consumer—a subject that we return to in Chapter Five. Often, this requires heavy investments to exploit scale economies, cut costs and prices, develop strong brands, and control the channels of distribution to the mass market.

The interesting thing in all of this is that the companies that end up winning the dominant design battle and succeed in scaling up small niches into mass markets are almost never the first into the new market. The success of consolidators is based on moving at the right time—and that is rarely first. Equally interesting is the fact that the early pioneers—those that helped create the market—rarely survive the consolidation of the market. Most disappear, never to be heard of again.

Why is that the case? In this chapter we explain this puzzling phenomenon by making the following points:

- The skills, mindsets, and structures needed for discovery and colonization are fundamentally different from those needed for consolidation and commercialization.
- Not only are the necessary skills for each activity different, they also conflict with each other. This means that firms that are good at colonization are unlikely to be good at consolidation. Very few firms are good at both of these activities.
- Big firms have the skills and mindsets to be good consolidators. Trying to teach them the skills of colonizing will not usually work because their existing skills conflict with many of the skills they need to develop.
- This implies that the challenge of becoming a successful colonizer is too formidable for big firms. They should leave this task to start-up firms that have the requisite skills and attitudes to succeed in that game.
- Big firms should focus on what they are good at—the consolidation of radical markets into mass markets. They can achieve this by adopting a network strategy with young start-up firms.

Different Skills for Discovery and Consolidation

Almost a hundred years ago, the famous economist Joseph Schumpeter pointed out the distinction between invention and innovation. Here, we'd like to make a related point: successful innovation is essentially a coupling process that requires the linking of two distinct activities: the discovery and initial testing of a new product (or service idea) that creates the initial market niche and the transformation of the idea from a little niche into a mass market. Both activities are obviously important and necessary for successful innovation, but there is no need for the same firm to do both. In fact, as noted, when it comes to radically new markets, the pioneers are rarely the ones that transform these markets into mass markets. Table 4.1 lists a number of new-to-the-world markets where this was the case.

Why are the first movers in radically new markets rarely able to translate early entry into a long-term market leadership position? It turns out that the reason is quite straightforward: the skills and mindsets needed for discovery and invention are not just different from those needed for commercialization, they also *conflict* with each other. This implies that firms that are good at invention are unlikely to be good at commercialization and vice versa.

Table 4.1. Two Types of Innovators: Idea Explorers and Market Creators.

Industry	Innovator That Came up with the Idea	Innovator That Created the Mass Market
35mm Cameras	Leica	Canon
ATMs	DeLaRue	IBM/NCR
Diapers	Chicopee Mills (J&J)	P&G
Personal Computers	Osborne/Apple	IBM
Online Bookselling	Charles Stack	Amazon
Online Brokerage	Net Investor	Schwab
VCRs	Ampex	JVC
Copiers	(Haloid) Xerox	Canon
CAT Scanners	EMI	GE
Videogames	Magnavox/Atari	Nintendo
Operating Systems	Digital Research	Microsoft
Pocket Calculators	Bowmar	TI
Mainframes	Atanasoff's ABC Computer	IBM

Source: Authors' research, plus Tellis and Golder (2002) and Schnaars (1994).

Some firms are natural *colonizers*, able to explore new technologies quickly and effectively, making the creative leap from technological possibility to something that meets consumer needs. What these firms are good at is creating new market niches. Other firms are natural *consolidators*. They are able to organize a market, turning a clever idea into something that can be economically manufactured and distributed to a mass market, something that reliably and regularly meets the promise that attracts consumers. However, very few firms are ever successful at both.

Effective Colonizers

What skills are needed for effective colonization? Given the technological and market turbulence of new markets, it should come as no surprise to learn that successful pioneering requires the ability to compete in unstructured and ever-changing environments. Early markets are characterized by high technological and customer uncertainty. New entrants come and go, constant experimentation is a way of life, and high turnover is the norm. Early markets are fluid and volatile places! Needless to say, most established companies would find such environments unattractive and inhospitable. In fact, the early colonizers of these markets display certain characteristics that are the exact opposite of those possessed by the companies that consolidate markets.

Colonists are enthusiasts. They understand the basic science and technology, and they are interested in pushing it as far as they can. They are willing to bet on seriously speculative projects that produce new products that are well beyond the frontier of current knowledge. They often assume that consumers share their enthusiasm for science and technology and value performance in the same way that they do.

Pioneers that colonize a market by exploring a new technology need to have skills rooted in a deep knowledge of that basic science and technology. They need to be flexible and adaptable so that they can respond to developments in the technology or in the market, and they need to be open to outside influences and to have internal mechanisms that facilitate the learning of technical information. Such firms do *not* need marketing skills—they often need to cultivate the attention of only a few lead users. They also do not need sophisticated production skills or the ability to produce in large volumes. Their organizations do not need to be very large or complex, and, hence, they also do not need organizational skills or the ability to build and monitor complex accounting, personnel, or service delivery systems. Colonists are, typically, quick-hit entrants, and their competitive advantage arises from their ability to be flexible and agile and to hit their target accurately.

Colonists are not great institution or empire builders. What they need is a culture that promotes experimentation and risk-taking; a loose and decentralized product structure with limited hierarchy; internal processes directed toward the generation, selection, and development of ideas; planning processes that are flexible and adaptable; incentives that reward new ideas and do not punish failures; people that are enthusiastic about new technologies and are eager to bet on seriously speculative projects in an effort to push the technological frontier beyond current knowledge; and small, entrepreneurial task-oriented teams that try out experiments without worrying about efficiencies or profits.

Effective Consolidators

Compare this set of skills needed for pioneering with the set of skills that consolidators need to transform niches into mass markets. To do so, consolidators need to win the dominant design battle and then scale up the market. This requires creating a large enough coalition of users (actual and potential) and encouraging complementary goods producers and rivals to adopt a particular product and business design so as to make competing designs seem much less attractive to all concerned. Creating a dominant design and consolidating a market around it is a formidable task. To do it successfully, a firm needs to make serious investments in production so that it can produce a high-quality product consistently and economically.

Furthermore, consolidators need to be able to help sway consumers and create the kind of consensus that would support their proposed dominant design. They need to be able to identify and then reach out to the many potential consumers who are ready to purchase the new product but are unwilling to shoulder the risk of choosing among the many prototypes that first appear on the market. Creating an organization that can serve a large and rapidly growing market is another set of skills consolidators need, if only to prevent any of their rivals from stealing a large share of the new market.

Consolidators are typically slow movers, and they ought to be. Assembling this list of skills is a formidable undertaking. It requires a disciplined organization with a clear market vision, a single-minded commitment, and an unwillingness to be too flexible. The organization must also be structured in such a way as to ensure that the very diverse set of skills needed to consolidate a market—production engineering, financial control, value chain management, and marketing—are effectively integrated. Most of the investments that are required involve substantial sunk costs and should not be undertaken lightly. Consolidators need, therefore, to be able to shoulder a substantial amount of financial risk. Furthermore, what starts the bandwagon rolling toward a particular dominant design is the presence of a major league champion. Indeed, the arrival in a market of one or more players of this type sends a clear signal to all concerned that the market is about to develop in new and very profitable ways.

Skills and Mindsets That Cannot Coexist

Clearly, the skill set necessary for effective colonizing is substantially different from that needed to consolidate markets. Table 4.2 compares the two sets of skills and mindsets needed to highlight just how different they are. But this by itself is not a major problem. Rather, the real problem arises because one set of skills cannot easily coexist with the other. In fact, they often conflict with each

Table 4.2. Characteristics of Colonizers and Consolidators.

Skills, Competencies, Mindsets and Attitudes Needed to Succeed as a Colonizer	Skills, Competencies, Mindsets and Attitudes Needed to Succeed as a Consolidator
Engineering or technology skills	Marketing, customer segmentation, and retailing skills
Emphasis on novelty, quality, and focus on lead users	Understanding of average user needs, good at spotting consensus
Young, restless, fascinated with science, technology, and the leading edge	More interested in making money than in developing the latest technological wonder
Roots in science	Commercial roots
Focus on technological achievements and creating the best-performing product	Focus on price and quality and willing to settle for a product that is "good enough"
Manage information network in science community	Manage network of feeder entrepreneurial firms
Entrepreneurs who prefer autonomy and freedom and do not want to work in a big company	Organization people, happy within the structures and constraints of a large organization
Fast, agile, risk-taking experimenters	People who defend the existing business and don't take unnecessary risks
Entrepreneurial culture	Functional organization, formal management control systems
First, fast mover	Judicious mover
Small is beautiful	Need resources to build the brand and distribution
Good at management of product design	Mastery of process engineering, procurement expertise, and mass-market management
A culture of innovation and experimentation	A culture of discipline and cost-control
Flexible	Disciplined
Short-term oriented	Long-term oriented
Fluid structures that allow easy flow of ideas and learning from mistakes	Managed hierarchy, focusing on mass marketing, customer segmentation, and manufacturing excellence

other to such a degree that any attempt to put the two together in the same organization is likely to create friction, disagreement, and inefficiency. A firm that attempts to adopt both sets of skills and mindsets runs the risk of messing up both activities and thus getting stuck in the middle.

Conflicts and trade-offs arise in three main areas.

Attitudes, Mindsets, and Cultural Conflicts. Perhaps the most serious conflict that arises is the cultural one. Colonists are technology enthusiasts. What they value is leading-edge research and technological breakthroughs. They enjoy playing with the latest technologies and their aspiration is to produce "the best"—even if it doesn't sell the most.

Consolidators, on the other hand, aim to produce a product that is good enough in terms of performance but cheap enough to attract the masses. Their emphasis is not on quality or technology but on price—they need to produce the product at a price low enough to make it attractive to the mass market. For example, the two-head video technology that JVC and Matsushita used for their products to capture the mass market for VCRs did not provide image quality as good as Ampex's four-head technology—but it was simpler and cheaper to make. Similarly, Kodak's celluloid film for taking pictures was far inferior to the prevailing dry-plate technology—but was much cheaper and Kodak used it as the platform to grow the huge amateur photography market.

The need to focus on costs rather than technology and product performance is anathema to the colonists, who value technological novelty over user needs. Shifting the organization's emphasis away from technology toward price and quality and diverting resources away from R&D toward manufacturing, distribution, and marketing is resisted by these young technologists. Serious internal conflicts and disagreements often ensue.

A second aspect of this cultural conflict gets manifested in the different ambitions and objectives of colonists and consolidators. Money is not the primary motivation for colonists. Instead, they prefer autonomy and freedom and do not want to work in a big company. They prefer to stay small and agile and they aspire to achieve technological breakthroughs. Consolidators, on the other hand, are more interested in making money than in developing the latest technological wonder. They are organization people, happy to work within the structures and constraints of a large organization. Needless to say, these kinds of people often cannot work well together!

Consider, for example, how the McDonald brothers reacted to Ray Kroc's proposal back in 1954 to form a national chain of hamburger restaurants. One of them expressed their feelings as follows: "See that big white house with the wide front porch? That's our home and we love it. We sit out on the porch in the evenings and watch the sunset and look down on our place here. It's peaceful. We don't need any more problems than we have in keeping this place going. More places, more problems. We are in a position to enjoy life now, and that's what we intend to do."[1]

In general, the organizational culture that colonists need is one that promotes experimentation and risk-taking with the implicit understanding that most of these experiments will fail. Failures are accepted and new ideas are rewarded. Technologists and innovators become heroes in these organizations and resources are always available even for the craziest of ideas. By contrast, the organizational culture that consolidators need is one that promotes cost-cutting and manufacturing excellence. Experiments are not encouraged, let alone promoted. Marketing and manufacturing people become the heroes of such organizations and everything must be approved or fall within the budget to be implemented. It is next to impossible for the same organization to succeed in creating a culture that supports both these extremes.

Structural Conflicts. Not only are the culture and mindsets necessary to be an effective colonist incompatible with those required to be a good consolidator but so are the structures and processes that need to be put in place in each organization. Colonists require a flat organization without hierarchical control. They need processes directed toward the generation, selection, and development of ideas and they require flexible planning processes with loose financial and operating controls. Work is done through task-oriented project teams and managers act as sponsors and coaches rather than operators.

By contrast, consolidators require a bureaucratic organization with clear hierarchy and transparent division of labor. They need distinct operating units that are controlled and coordinated by top management. And they require well-thought-out systems and operating controls that keep a tight lid on costs while collecting and exploiting valuable customer information for marketing purposes.

The heart of the problem is that colonizers are experimenters while consolidators are integrators. Mastering a new science or technology and bringing it to market in the form of a new good is a lot like groping in the dark. Firms that undertake such activities need to be able to change direction quickly and run on blind faith. Formal structures are much less useful than frameworks (or paradigms) in organizing such activities. By contrast, consolidation requires bringing together many quite different skills to make the basic business design work. This requires planning and control, not experimentation! It is hard to tolerate creativity in such organizations—it is difficult enough to get people to work toward the same goal, and taking time off to debate what that goal ought to be is likely to be counterproductive. Colonists need to give project teams the freedom to go where they think is best; consolidators need to rein in project teams to ensure that what they are doing meshes well with what other teams in the same organization or in alliance partner organizations are doing.

One can only imagine the complexity of trying to set up a structure that performs both these sets of activities in an efficient manner! Although one could certainly argue that in theory such a structure could be put in place, doing so must be next to impossible in practice—and so it has proved for most of the firms that have tried.

Incentives and Organizational Conflicts. Once a company moves from creating to growing a market, not only do the resource requirements become substantially greater, but—what is more important—the organizational problems and conflicts multiply.

To begin with, recall from Chapter Two that radical innovations tend to be disruptive for both consumers and producers. For firms that have carefully built up businesses around existing products, radical innovations can be a major threat because they create new markets that cannibalize existing products and undermine the prevailing competences and complementary assets of the winning firms. They also demand new and sometimes rather risky investments in doing new things. For managers whose incentives are tied to the performance of existing markets, the new radical markets are a threat that has to be neutralized. Asking them to either promote the growth of the new markets or support their colleagues who are trying to do so is a strategy that's bound to fail.

Furthermore, even if a radically new market is successful in getting off the ground, established firms will not be particularly enthusiastic in going after it. This is because all new ideas start out as small, risky, uncertain, and low-margin businesses. As a result, it is difficult to gain support or long-term commitment from the organization of an established competitor. Exactly because these new markets are so small relative to the mainstream business, they are not particularly attractive to big, established companies. Even managers in these established companies who want to do something about the new markets find it difficult to justify investment in them on economic grounds. As long as they are able to retain their mainstream customers in their existing business, they are unwilling to invest significant resources in the new market. Not surprisingly, it is rare to find new and radical markets being created by established companies. It is usually an entrepreneur or a new market entrant that introduces the innovations that create the new market.

Finally, compared to the traditional business, new markets have different key success factors and as a result require a different combination of tailored activities on the part of the firm. These new activities are incompatible with the company's existing set of activities because of various trade-offs that exist between the two ways of doing business.

For example, trade-offs might arise from inconsistencies in a company's image or reputation. Firms that try to offer at the same time two different kinds of value that are not consistent with each other run the risk of jeopardizing their existing image and reputation. Similarly, trade-offs might occur because the tailored activities that a firm needs to compete in its existing position are incompatible with the activities needed in the new market. Finally, trade-offs might arise due to the organizational limits that a firm might face in trying to internally coordinate and control incompatible sets of activities in two different markets—its mature existing market and the new young market.

The fact that the skills needed to be an effective colonist conflict with the skills that consolidators need to scale up a market makes it extremely difficult for any given firm to be effective at colonization and consolidation simultaneously. The story of how Xerox was the first firm to develop a working model of the laser printer but then lost the market to IBM and HP vividly illustrates these organizational conflicts. Despite constant resistance from his colleagues at Xerox's main research laboratories at Webster, Gary Starkweather persisted in experimenting with the laser printer in the early 1960s. His prototype laser printer met with ridicule and his boss threatened to take away his people unless he stopped experimenting. In frustration, he asked for transfer to Xerox's PARC facility, where he found fellow visionaries who were as excited about new technologies as he was. In two years, he developed a working prototype of the laser printer. Unfortunately, it took Xerox even more time to recognize the potential of the new product. It remained in development for seven more years before it was finally introduced in 1977 as the Xerox 9700.

Getting Stuck in the Middle

Trying to set up structures, cultures, and processes that facilitate colonization on one hand and consolidation on the other is a very difficult task. The cultures needed for each activity conflict with each other. The incentives and investment horizons needed to do each activity well are fundamentally different and cannot coexist. The attitudes toward risk are so different that the same firm will find it virtually impossible to do both activities at the same time. Even the mindsets and behaviors needed for each activity are so incompatible that coexistence is next to impossible. It's not that the task is totally impossible but chances are that most companies that attempt to do it will find themselves stuck in the middle.

The example of Lotus, now part of IBM, highlights how difficult it is to combine the two types of organizations.[2] After its initial success with its "killer application" (Lotus 1-2-3), Lotus brought in experienced professional managers to guide it forward. It soon discovered, however, that the structures and processes that the mature Lotus had put in place to function effectively were inhibiting innovation. In a classic experiment to demonstrate this, top managers put together the résumés of the first forty people to join the company, disguised their names, and put them into the applicant group. Not one of these applicants was called for an interview! It appears that the MBA-type professional managers that ran the established Lotus considered the wacky risk-takers that had created Lotus as too deviant from the current culture of Lotus to warrant even an interview.

Contemporary business is filled with examples that support the distinctions between colonization and consolidation skills. Apple Computer pioneered the home PC market, but was unable to scale it up. However, Apple's competencies may yet allow it to win as an online music and entertainment distribution company, expanding a niche that industry pioneer Real Networks helped invent but has been unable to scale-up profitably. Microsoft might appear to be both colonizer and consolidator; in fact, though, the company's expertise is in following and growing markets uncovered by others, whether in word processing programs (Microsoft Word versus WordPerfect), spreadsheets (Excel versus Lotus), operating systems (Windows versus Mac OS), or other products.

There are, of course, exceptions to this rule. 3M was successful in both discovering and commercializing the Post-it note. But such cases are rare. If we are careful in correctly identifying who the early pioneers in new radical markets truly are, we will soon see that these pioneers are not the ones that scaled up the new market.

Do You Have to Be Stuck in the Middle?

This, of course, raises an interesting dilemma for established companies. Given the skills, competences, attitudes, and cultures that they possess, it should come as no surprise to learn that these are exactly the firms that are good at consolidation. They are the ones that have the necessary financial resources, market power, reputation, brand-building skills, and manufacturing and marketing expertise that consolidation of markets requires. On the other hand, established firms are usually not very good at colonization. They lack the basic science knowledge and entrepreneurial skills to succeed when it comes to radical innovation. They do not have the necessary cultures or structures to succeed in the turbulent environments of new radical markets. And they lack the attitudes and mindsets that are required for pioneering.

Given this basic fact, what options are available to established companies that want to create new-to-the-world markets?

The Option of Radical Cultural Change. The first and most obvious option is to attempt to learn or adopt the skills and attitudes of a colonist. In fact, much of the advice of the last few years by academics and consultants has been targeted at making established companies better at creating new markets by developing the cultures and structures of the younger start-up firms. For example, some academics have proposed ideas such as making the strategy process democratic and "bringing Silicon Valley inside the organization" as ingredients to radical innovation. Others have argued that corporations could learn from the success of the capitalist system by importing into their organizations those features of capitalism—decentralized allocation of resources, multiple sources of financing, and constant experimentation—that promote innovation in the wider economy.

Unfortunately, these suggestions are unlikely to do much good. The skills and attitudes that large, established companies currently have (and need) to compete successfully in their mature businesses cannot easily coexist with the skills and competences needed for colonizing new radical markets. This means that attempting to incorporate the skills of colonization in the existing organization can produce one of only two outcomes. Either the existing culture and attitudes reject the new transplants, very much the way an organism rejects a transplanted foreign organ; or the transplanted skills and attitudes take over and destroy the very things that have made the established firm a success (and that it still needs to be successful in its existing business). Either way, the outcome is unpalatable!

Think about it. Even a cursory comparison of the markets that established competitors inhabit with markets that have just been created should alert us to the fact that these are wildly different beasts. Is it sensible to expect the same organization to develop the requisite skills and attitudes to manage such extremes effectively? As far back as 1961, academics were making the point that such a task is close to impossible.[3]

A variant of this option builds on the argument that the skills of colonizing and consolidation can coexist if the company is successful in creating an *ambidextrous* organizational infrastructure. This is an organization that has successfully put in place multiple, contradictory structures, processes, and cultures within the same organizational infrastructure. By developing strong shared values and by putting in charge managers capable of managing variety and ambiguity, ambidextrous organizations can successfully balance the conflicting demands that the simultaneous pursuit of colonization and consolidation would place on them.

This is admirable, and we do not deny that such organizations do exist—but we also believe that they are few and far between. Only a small minority of farsighted firms can claim to be ambidextrous. Most firms that try to do so will probably fail. Furthermore, there is no reason why colonization ought to happen in the same organization as consolidation does, and there is every reason to think that it might be more sensible for consolidators to manage colonization outside their organization.

The Option of Separation.   Recognizing how difficult it is for the skills of colonizing to coexist with the skills of consolidation, other academics have proposed that established firms should separate the pioneering activity in an independent unit or division (internal venture). Although this solution was offered primarily to companies facing the challenge of disruptive strategic innovation, it is equally applicable to radical innovation.

The rationale for this solution is quite straightforward. The established organization is too old and too efficiency-driven to accommodate a youthful, entrepreneurial venture in its existing infrastructure. Even worse, the presence of conflicts means that the existing organization and its managers will often find that the new radical market is growing at their expense. They will therefore have incentives to constrain it or even kill it. Therefore, by keeping the two businesses separate, you prevent the company's existing processes and culture from suffocating the new business. The new unit can develop its own culture, processes, and strategy without interference from the parent company. It can also manage its business as it sees fit without being suffocated by the managers of the established company, who see cannibalization threats and channel conflicts at every turn.

Resorting to a separate organizational entity is certainly a viable option and it is one that several companies have used. The most famous example of this strategy is IBM's decision to set up its PC organization in Boca Raton, Florida, purposely away from the established IBM organization and away from corporate interference.

Another example is Nestlé's decision to set up a separate unit called Nespresso to sell espresso coffee to young urban professionals in the early 1990s. Nestlé set up the new unit in a totally different town in Switzerland and gave it the freedom and autonomy to compete in its market as it saw fit. The strategy proved to be a great success and Nespresso is now a profitable unit within Nestlé.

Sensible as this strategy might be, the separation solution is not without problems and risks. Perhaps the biggest cost of keeping the two businesses separate is failure to exploit synergies between the two. For example, a recent study on the subject has concluded, "The simple injunction to cordon off new businesses is too narrow. Although ventures do need space to develop, strict separation can prevent them from obtaining invaluable resources and rob their parents of the vitality they can generate."[4] Similarly, another study on the issue of separation found that "spinoffs often enable faster action early on but they later have difficulty achieving true staying power in the market. Even worse, by launching a spinoff, a company often creates conditions that make future integration very difficult."[5]

Perhaps the strongest case against the separation strategy is to be found in the arguments of Chapter Two: the innovation process that creates new-to-the-world markets cannot be easily replicated inside the R&D facility of the modern corporation, and the early pioneers of new markets do not usually survive the consolidation of these markets. Given these facts, why should a big firm adopt a separation strategy so as to rush into a market that it did not create? And why should it be the pioneer that will likely lose out to a consolidator later in the evolution of the new market? Will it not be better off simply waiting for somebody else to create the new markets and then move in at the right time to consolidate them by utilizing its existing competences?

It is for these reasons that recent academic work has proposed an "open-innovation" model for companies that want to create radical new technologies. The idea is to find ways to access and exploit outside knowledge and research while liberating internal expertise for others' use. A variant of this strategy for radical new markets is to outsource colonization altogether. This is the strategy that leverages the big firms' strengths and this is the strategy that we describe next.

Outsourcing Colonization. A final option—and the one that most people have ignored—is to recognize that the challenge of becoming a successful colonizer is too formidable for established firms. They should leave this task to the market—the zillions of small start-up firms around the world that have the requisite skills and attitudes to succeed at this game. Established firms should, instead, concentrate on what they are good at—which is to consolidate young markets into big mass markets. After all, big firms have established one thing in their history: they are good at consolidating new markets. And being a consolidator has given them access to first-mover advantages—advantages that the vast majority of pioneers never got close to realizing.

A similar specialization of labor has been proposed by other researchers as well. For example, a recent article on the subject has argued:[6]

It does seem that some companies, and some people, are better at reconnaissance [scouting out new market opportunities and technological possibilities] than others. They pan for gold in the same streams as many before them but come back with the nuggets no one else spotted. So shouldn't we study those experts closely to find out how they do it—and then codify their secrets into a replicable process that we can impose on our own organizations? We used to think so. . . . But increasingly, our attitude is shifting. We now warn companies, "Don't try this at home." Like many activities that involve talent and tacit learning, reconnaissance requires an inherent feel for the work and lots of practice. Not many companies can claim that inherent strength; nor can they devote much time to practicing, given that their day-to-day work is exploitation, not exploration.

Practically speaking, what this means is that instead of spending valuable resources and managerial talent at growing new radical businesses inside, established companies should aim to create, sustain, and nurture a network of feeder firms—of young, entrepreneurial firms busily colonizing new niches. Through its business development function, the established company could serve as a venture capitalist to these feeder firms. Alternatively, it could develop formal strategic alliances with them or even maintain minority equity stakes in them. Then, when it is time to consolidate the market, it could build a new mass-market business on the platform that the best and most promising of these feeder firms have provided.

Such a specialization of labor already exists in creative industries such as the theater, movies, book publishing, and the visual and performing arts. Firms in such industries are either small-scale pickers that concentrate on the selection and development of new creative talent or large-scale promoters that undertake the packaging and widespread distribution of established creative goods. Similarly, many commentators have argued that a small but rapidly growing industry has emerged, made up of companies whose specialty is exploration. Mature firms are increasingly outsourcing their exploration needs to these firms, choosing to focus their attention on growing the ideas into mass markets. Strategically outsourcing innovation is now an accepted practice in a number of industries, including pharmaceuticals, financial services, computers, telecommunications, and energy systems.

Such a network strategy has several advantages over the "grow it inside" strategy: it allows the firm to cover more technologies and more market niches; it enables the feeder firms to compete with one another while allowing the parent company to benchmark one against the other; it is easier to manage because it bypasses all the problems of trying to manage two conflicting businesses simultaneously; and it has all the traditional benefits of outsourcing.[7]

Avoiding Getting Stuck in the Middle

Therefore, the right way forward for established, mature firms is not to build their own new businesses inside and then consolidate them when the time is right. Rather, they should maintain and manage a feeder system of colonizer businesses—very much what pharmaceutical companies are doing with biotech and what Unilever and P&G are doing with new consumer products. Then, when the time is right, they should move in for consolidation and scaling up. This is the area where the established corporation has unique advantages over start-up firms. This, therefore, is the area where it should focus its attention.

We are aware that this cuts against the grain of much of the thinking of the last few years, which aimed to make established corporations more entrepreneurial by developing the cultures and structures of the younger start-up firms. In our view, this is misplaced advice. It's like advising a seventy-year-old man how to train to win at the next Olympics—it simply won't happen! What the established market leaders ought to focus on is gaining access to the ideas generated by the start-up firms and then scaling them up to create mass markets. It seems to us that by trying to be ambidextrous, established companies risk being stuck in the middle. What they need to do is focus on the area where they have an advantage—and that is on consolidating good new ideas drawn from niche markets into new and valuable mass markets.

Final Thoughts

Over the past twenty years, academics and consultants have developed a wealth of ideas to make big, established firms more entrepreneurial. By encouraging them to adopt the cultures and structures of younger start-up firms, we had hoped to make the established firms as innovative as their younger counterparts. Unfortunately, despite all the advice and good intentions, it is very rare to find a big, established company among the firms that create new radical markets—most (though not all) innovations that create new radical markets seem to originate from small start-up firms.

It's not that the advice is bad! If we ignore who the recipient of the advice is for a moment, we cannot but marvel at the logic of the advice. For example, who could argue with proposals to make the strategy process democratic or bring capitalism inside a firm? And who could dispute the fact that big, established companies can be so bureaucratic and inflexible at times that they could do with some shaking up and nontraditional thinking? These are all sensible and creative ideas. But they will not help established companies create new radical markets!

The problem is not that established firms do not agree with these ideas or that they do not want to adopt them. On the contrary, they will find our recommendations (such as developing cultures that encourage experimentation or making their strategy process democratic or even developing a self-cannibalizing attitude) constructive and useful. But despite agreeing with all this, they probably will not succeed in adopting these attitudes and cultures. This is because they already have a set of skills and attitudes that they need to successfully compete in their existing businesses. This set of skills and attitudes makes them good at exploitation and consolidation, which is exactly what they need to do well in their mature businesses. Asking them to also adopt a set of skills and attitudes that will make them good colonizers is asking too much. The skills and attitudes needed for colonization coexist poorly with the skills and attitudes needed for consolidation—they often conflict with each other. Attempting to bring on board the skills of colonization will most likely provoke a reaction from the organization. The organization's antibodies will go to work and the new skills and attitudes will be rejected as unwanted foreign organs.

But not all is dire for big, established firms! In this chapter, we argued that their skills, mindsets, and attitudes are ideal for the strategy of consolidation—for taking the new market niches developed by others and scaling them up into mass markets. This implies that instead of telling established companies how to create new markets, we should be advising them how to scale up niche markets into big mass markets. We turn to this topic in the next chapter.

Chapter Five

From Colonization to Consolidation

In October 2003, in a press release accompanying the company's annual meeting, Procter & Gamble Chairman and Chief Executive A.G. Lafley said: "Our vision is that 50 percent of all P&G discovery and invention could come from outside the company." The target was ambitious: in 2002, only one-fifth of new ideas put into development by P&G came from the outside. But the company hoped that by working with partners, including other public companies, start-ups, and universities, outside innovation would ultimately form half its portfolio.

The desire and goal by P&G to outsource half of its discovery and invention should not come as a surprise to those readers who followed the arguments of Chapter Four closely. In that chapter, we proposed that big, established firms do not have to be actively involved in both colonizing and consolidating new radical markets. Instead, we suggested that given their skills and attitudes, they might be better off if they focused on consolidating radical markets by exploiting the pioneering efforts of others. The decision by Procter & Gamble to outsource half of its discovery and invention is a practical example of what we are recommending for all big, established companies.

Unfortunately, few companies have the courage to do what P&G is attempting to do. Many firms claim that if they separated discovery from consolidation, they might not be able to take advantage of the market when it grows. After all, aren't the discoverers the ones that dominate the markets that they discover and don't first movers enjoy enormous advantages over latecomers? The answer, as we have repeatedly stated in this book, is no! When it comes to radically new markets, discovery and consolidation are essentially different activities best undertaken by different firms.

Other firms shy away from the idea, claiming that they'd rather keep 100 percent of the spoils than share them with another firm. Unfortunately this argument is based on flawed logic. Yes, we would all prefer to keep all the spoils rather than share them—but without sharing, there may be no spoils at all! Yet others are afraid that without controlling R&D they cannot guarantee proprietary access to it. This is a valid concern, but again, as we argued in Chapter Two, the innovation process that creates radically new markets is not one that a single firm can control in its laboratory. In any case, the purpose of maintaining a network of start-up firms is to have access to the latest technology. As long as the relationship with smaller firms is based on trust and win-win outcomes, established firms can have access to the technology developed by smaller firms in return for helping the smaller firms scale up the market.[1]

The real obstacle to outsourcing the discovery of new radical markets is cultural. While everybody knows and celebrates what inventors and pioneers do, few people seem to appreciate that consolidation is equally innovative, if not more so. Consider, for example, the personal computer industry. Who do you regard as more innovative in this industry—Apple or IBM? If your mind thinks of machines and their features and you believe that innovation is all about introducing new and exciting products, the answer is a no-brainer—Apple is the innovator. However, which of these two firms do you think is responsible for the major growth and development of the PC market that occurred in the early 1980s? Are you confident that the business as it is today would have come about quite as quickly and quite as effectively if IBM had decided to focus its business on mainframes? Wasn't the IBM PC an innovation of substance, even if it contained nothing particularly new or breathtaking from a technology point of view?

There has long been a cultural and management bias in favor of discovery. We all aspire to become a modern-day Christopher Columbus or Thomas Edison—the pioneer, the inventor, the company that discovers the industries of the future—forgetting that this is only half the story. A natural by-product of this bias is that most of the advice that academics and consultants give companies to make them more innovative is primarily advice on how companies can become better at *creation*—discovering something new, testing it in the market, and, if successful, creating a new market niche. There is precious little advice on how companies could become better at scaling up.

This is unfortunate because scaling up a market is not only as creative and innovative as creating the market in the first place, it's also more rewarding financially. In this chapter, we show how established firms could scale up newly created markets by making the following points:

- What creates a radically new market is superb technology embedded in a new product—but what creates the mass market is an *economically priced* product. Consolidators grow the market by delivering a product that is not necessarily the best—it is just good enough—but it is superior to all others in value for money.

- To win the mass market, a product must win consumer consensus as the dominant design. Consolidators achieve this by creating a consumer bandwagon.

- Given the high customer uncertainty that prevails in new markets, consolidators must build confidence in the new product so as to reduce the customers' risk when they adopt the new product.

- Consolidators must also build a distribution system that can reach the mass market. They could either build this from scratch or use their market power to get existing distributors to adopt the new product.

- Finally, for new radical products to grow, they require the support of complementary goods. Consolidators find ways to not only grow their own markets but support the growth of complementary goods.

The skills and competences needed to do all this reside within the big, established corporation. Rather than attempt to become something that they cannot (that is, colonists), big, established firms are better off focusing on something that they have the competences for (that is, consolidation of new markets).

Consolidation Is King

The market for online services was created by CompuServe in 1979 with the provision of its first offering, the CompuServe information service. Over time, CompuServe used its pioneering efforts in video-tex technology to enable users to not only access information but also perform banking and shopping transactions from their homes. Additional services such as e-mail, electronic bulletin boards, and forums were added throughout the 1980s. As the market grew, it attracted new competitors such as AOL and Prodigy. By 1990, the market for online services had about one million subscribers and CompuServe was its clear leader.

Then, suddenly and without warning, the market simply exploded: while it took more than ten years for the market to grow to one million subscribers, it took only another seven for the market to increase ten times, to more than 10 million subscribers by the start of 1998. By then, AOL had emerged as the clear leader, having acquired CompuServe's subscriber base and content operations in February 1998.

What happened? Specifically, what did AOL do that allowed it to not only grow the market in such an exponential manner, but also to emerge as the clear winner (at least so far)? The answer is that AOL, like any good consolidator, had scaled up the new market by following a combination of the following five strategies.

Emphasizing Different Product Attributes

The early pioneers that rush to colonize a new market do so by emphasizing the *technical* attributes of the product. Most of the time, this happens simply because the entrepreneurs who created the company are engineers. It is their technical and engineering skills that allowed them to translate a certain technology into a product, and it is the functionality of this product that attracts the early consumers.

You see this emphasis on the technical attributes of the product in the early phases of all young markets. For example, Xerox sold its copiers by emphasizing their functionality and speed; Ampex sold its VCRs on the quality of their recording; Leica sold its cameras on the quality of their lenses, which guaranteed quality pictures; Cuisinart sold its food processors by focusing on its engineering skills, which translated into high-quality machines; and Apple sold its handheld computer on its breakthrough hand-writing-recognition software.

This emphasis on the technical aspects and functionality of the product early on in the evolution of a new market is understandable. To begin with, the product comes into being because it satisfies a certain customer need. Unless it has the necessary technical features to meet this need, it will not succeed. Second, the entrepreneurs who created the product are usually engineers—they are the ones who understand the technology and toil for years to translate it into a workable product. Their natural inclination is to emphasize the things they know and the things they believe make their product better than other products. Third, at the start of any new market, the performance of early products is still below what customers expect or want. This means that a competitor that invests in improving the performance of its product to bring its level closer to what customers want will benefit from such investment. This implies that competition in the early stages of the market is based on product features and performance—early pioneers compete against each other by adding functionality to their products.

The efforts of these early pioneers create the early market niche. The consumers that rush to purchase the new product tend to be technology enthusiasts or early adopters. They don't particularly mind that the product is flawed or expensive—they just want to get their hands on the new toy in the market. Obviously, these early adopters represent only a small fraction of the population. There-fore, by definition, the early pioneers are targeting a niche market.

It is at this stage that consolidators move in and steal the market away. What they do is shift the basis of competition from technical performance to other product attributes such as quality and price. They do this by cutting the price of the product to a mass-market level while at the same time improving the quality of the product to make it acceptable to the average consumer. All of a sudden, the product becomes attractive to the mass market and rapid growth follows.[2] Exhibit 5.1 shows that the tactic of shifting the emphasis from the technical attributes of the product to price and quality is something that consolidators have used in industry after industry. The evolution of the disposable diaper market in the U.S. illustrates this point well.

Most people think that Procter & Gamble pioneered the dis-posable diaper market by introducing Pampers in 1961. The truth is that although P&G was the first to popularize the disposable dia-per to the mass market, credit for pioneering the first disposable diaper must go to Chicopee Mills, a unit of Johnson & Johnson. Chicopee Mills introduced the first disposable diaper—Chux—as early as 1932. Two other providers, Sears and Montgomery Ward, also launched disposable diapers before P&G did. However, these products did not prove long-term successes and failed to capture the public's imagination.

By 1956, disposable diapers accounted for only 1 percent of dia-per changes in the United States. The main reason was their high cost (about 9 cents per unit), which was more than double what laundry service cost (and much more costly than home washing). Another reason was the product's performance: not only did the diapers come with no attachment tapes, which meant that they had to be anchored with traditional safety pins, but even worse, their absorbent core was made of several layers of tissue paper, which led to a high leakage rate. Thus consumers treated dispos-able diapers as a luxury item to be used only on special occasions (such as traveling with babies).

Exhibit 5.1. Scaling Up a Market by Emphasizing Different Product Attributes.

Industry	Early Pioneers	Product Attributes Emphasized by Pioneers	Firms Scaling Up the Market	Product Attributes Emphasized by Scaling-Up Firms
Photocopying	(Haloid) Xerox and 3M	Speed and quality of copying	Canon	Price, size, quality
Handheld computers	Apple (Newton)	Writing recognition software, features	Palm (3Com)	Price, size, and PC synchronization
Online brokerage	K. Aufhauser, Security APL, and Howe Barnes	Convenience	Charles Schwab	Price, convenience, speed of execution
Portable computers	Osborne and Apple	Technology, features	IBM	Price, size
Video recorders	Ampex	High-quality recording	JVC and Sony	Price, size, weight
Online bookselling	Books.com, Charles Stack, and clbooks.com	Convenience	Amazon.com	Availability, convenience, price
Motorcycles	Triumph and Harley-Davidson	Speed and power	Honda	Size and price
35mm cameras	Leica	Quality (of lenses and pictures), engineering	Canon and Nikon	Price, ease of use
Microwave ovens	Tappan Stove Co., Raytheon, and Litton	Speed and quality	Panasonic, Sharp, and Samsung	Price
Internet service provider	CompuServe	Technology, info content, speed, and features	AOL	Ease of use, price
Food processors	Cuisinart	Speed, features, quality	Black & Decker	Price
Shaving razors	Cutthroat Razors and Autostrop Safety Razor Co.	High-grade steel for lifetime of sharpening	Gillette	Disposable blade, price, ease of use
Pocket calculators	Bowmar	Speed, features, ease of use	Texas Instruments	Price
Disposable diapers	Chicopee Mills (J&J)	Ease of use	P&G	Price, ease of use
Fax machines	Xerox	Quality and speed	Sharp	Price, ease of use

Pampers owes its existence to Victor Mills, a chemical engineer working for P&G. In 1956, the company acquired a paper pulp plant and Mills's team of engineers took on the job of figuring out what to do with it. A grandfather by then, Mills remembered how much he hated changing diapers and it occurred to him that using cellulose fibers instead of paper would vastly improve the performance of a diaper. The challenge, however, was how to use this idea to design an acceptable disposable diaper for the mass market at a reasonable price. On the design front, the diaper had to be soft enough to be comfortable, yet strong enough not to disintegrate when wet. On the price front, the firm would need to devise an efficient manufacturing process that would allow it to manufacture the diaper cheaply enough to make it price-attractive for the average consumer.

It took five years of research before the first Pampers was finally launched in 1961. The initial test market was not successful: even though the product was rated highly by consumers, it was still too expensive for most of them. It took another five years of research and improvements in manufacturing technology before P&G was able to reduce the unit price far enough to stimulate the mass market. Drawing upon its vast experience in grocery marketing and its early research efforts, P&G had set as a target a retail price of 6.2 cents per diaper. This meant that manufacturing costs had to be around 3 cents, something that entailed significant reductions in raw material costs and a more efficient manufacturing process.

It was only when P&G succeeded in producing high-quality diapers at a cost of 3.5 cents a unit that Pampers was finally given a national rollout in 1966 (at the retail price of 5.5 cents per diaper). At such a low price, Pampers became an instant success. The U.S. disposable diaper market grew from $10 million in 1966 to $370 million by 1973 and demand for the product was so high that the firm struggled to satisfy it. The success of Pampers was so overwhelming that the pioneer of this market—Johnson & Johnson—withdrew its brand (Chux) from the market and focused on a private label. By 1981, J&J withdrew from the branded market completely.

This example shows how a late entrant scaled up and captured the market not only by cutting the price of the product but also by improving its quality. The irony is that in many cases, a late entrant can still capture the market even when its product is not as good as the products of the early pioneers. It is instructive to understand why that happens.

As we argued earlier, the efforts of the early pioneers create the early market niche. Unfortunately for them, two things follow that set the stage for their downfall. First, as a result of their investments in improving the performance of the product, the product could actually improve to performance levels that surpass customer needs. At that stage, any additional investments to improve the performance of the product further are not really necessary. But the early pioneers cannot help it! Their engineering cultures go to work and sure enough, more and more money goes into R&D to improve the product still further. All this happens even though they know full well that the customers do not need nor will they ever use the added functionality. (For example, how many people really care if their photocopier can actually make 250 copies per minute rather than 100?)

Overengineering of the product is linked to the second change taking place: the extra investments and incremental additions to the product's performance do not come free. The rising costs lead to rising prices. The high price, in turn, means that only a small segment made up of technology enthusiasts and early adopters find the product attractive enough to buy.

The combination of these two factors is what gives consolidators their chance to move in. They know that all they have to do is produce a product that is "good enough" in performance but cheaper than what is on the market now. Their product may not be as good as the product of the pioneers but this does not really matter. The *early adopters* are not attracted to these technically inferior products—but the *average consumers* are! To them, this is a product that is good enough and cheap. Over time, the consolidators may improve the performance of their product to such an extent that even technically astute customers begin to find it attractive (and so switch). But this is not absolutely necessary. As long as they control the mass market, the consolidators are happy to leave a few little niches for other competitors to feed on. Their overriding objective is to make a product that is not necessarily the best—just one that is good enough in performance and superior in price.

The story of how Palm conquered the handheld computer market illustrates this point well. Apple created the market by introducing the Newton in August 1993. Palm followed soon after with the introduction of the Palm Zoomer in October 1993. Both products flopped in the market—not only did they have poor handwriting recognition, they were also expensive, heavy, and overburdened with PC functions (like spreadsheet software and printing) that made them slow.

By the mid-1990s, Palm was really at a dead end. It was then that it got acquired by US Robotics—a much bigger firm with financial and marketing clout. The following year the Palm Pilot was introduced, and it proved to be a hit with consumers. The infusion of resources, established distribution outlets, and branding expertise from the bigger parent certainly helped Palm scale up the PDA market at last. But what's of interest here is the nature of the product that allowed Palm to achieve such a feat.

If we were to compare the Apple Newton with the Palm Pilot, it is safe to suggest that the Newton was a much more sophisticated product in technical terms. And that's exactly the point! The Newton was like a scaled-down PC, loaded with all kinds of software applications. By contrast, the Pilot was conceived as an *accessory* to the PC, to be used primarily as an organizer with connectivity to the PC. It was also simple and fast and, more important, cheap ($299). The Pilot was a huge triumph. It was less sophisticated than the Newton but was exactly what the mass market wanted and needed!

By the turn of the century, Palm controlled more than 70 percent of the market. In the years that followed the Palm Pilot's introduction, Microsoft developed its own operating system for handheld computers—the Windows CE—and hardware vendors such as HP, Casio, and Philips entered the handheld market carrying this OS. Repeated attempts by Microsoft to make inroads in this market by adding more features and more memory have failed. Microsoft's motto of "more is better" has come up against Palm's "smaller, faster, cheaper"—and so far, Palm is winning.

Both the Palm and the P&G examples highlight the importance of a low price in scaling up a market. But it is one thing to aim for a low price and another to actually deliver it. That too requires innovation.

Driving Costs Down

To win on price, consolidators need to drive their costs down to levels that the early pioneering firms cannot match. The most effective way to do this is to gain market share quickly and so achieve economies of scale. There are, obviously, many ways to do this, but remember—we are at that stage in the evolution of the market when lots of pioneers compete on numerous product designs and a dominant design has yet to emerge. This means that the way to quickly gain market share is to ensure that your product wins consumer consensus as the dominant design. In the next section, we explore how to achieve this by creating consumer bandwagons.

Creating bandwagon effects that win market share is an effective way for consolidators to drive down their costs and ambush the early pioneers through low prices. But there are many other ways to cut costs. For example, designing the product in a way that makes it easy (or cheap) to manufacture, investing in manufacturing capacity, and developing efficient supply chains and logistics are equally effective cost-cutting strategies. When the strategy of low prices is combined with other clever marketing or strategic moves, the combined effect could be devastating for the early pioneers. Consider, for example, the case of Intel in the development of chips for mobile computers.

In the late 1990s, Silicon Valley firm Transmeta promised to revolutionize mobile computing by introducing microprocessor chips for portable computers that generated far less heat and consumed less power than anything Intel had to offer. This would mean longer battery life for portable computers. Furthermore, the chips themselves could be designed into computers in shapes and sizes that hadn't previously been possible. Transmeta had been working in total secrecy for years, and fueling the frenzy was one of its lead software engineers, Linus Torvalds, who was already famous for developing the core of the Linux operating system (a more flexible alternative to Windows).

Transmeta introduced the Crusoe chip in January 2000. Compared to existing designs, the Crusoe had fewer transistors which allowed it to consume less power and therefore produce less heat. Every major newspaper in the United States and many broadcast networks covered the press conference at which the Crusoe chip was presented.

The hype was short-lived. Crusoe was not much of a commercial success because it was mainly used only by notebook PC manufacturers in Japan and by Hewlett-Packard for its tablet PC. However, Transmeta's designs were sufficiently innovative to spur both Intel and AMD (both already established players in the chip industry) into action. In early 2003, three years after Crusoe was released, Intel revealed its own Centrino chip platform designed to throttle back chip speeds to preserve power.

Centrino quickly became a success and spurred notebook sales, something that Transmeta failed to achieve. Why? One reason is the Crusoe's failure to deliver adequate processing power (speed) despite drawing significantly less power from computer batteries. By contrast, the Centrino delivered much higher performance speed (up to 1.6 GHz) while also achieving comparably low power consumption levels and thus a longer battery life. Another reason was the huge marketing budget that Intel devoted to the launch of the Centrino. At $300 million, Intel's marketing muscle was four times what Transmeta could afford.

A third reason was Intel's clever strategy of bundling its chip with other complementary features. The Centrino mobile platform combined the aforementioned processor features with a Pentium M mobile processor, related chipsets, and a WLAN Intel adapter. Only notebook companies that used all three of these components were allowed to use the Centrino brand name. This restriction forced many notebook manufacturers to embrace Centrino because it combined many popular features under a very strong brand name, that of Intel.

A final reason for the Centrino's success has to do with Intel's pricing strategy. Because of its size, Intel could afford to sell its chips less expensively than it normally would in order to gain a foothold in a given market. Transmeta matched the Intel low prices but given its small size and the fact that its three-year technological lead was built upon huge R&D expenses and ongoing losses, the company could not afford a prolonged price war. In October 2003, Transmeta launched its Efficeon processor but has so far failed to win any major contracts with notebook manufacturers. It is conceivable that the rapid notebook market growth that Centrino has brought about may allow Transmeta some room to survive. However, a more likely outcome is that Transmeta will be taken over by one of its bigger and more established competitors.

Winning the Dominant Design Race

Consolidation of a market cannot take place unless a dominant design emerges. For a dominant design to become established, a consensus must form among consumers that a particular design is the right one. Those aspiring to scale up a market must find ways to create a bandwagon that ensures the selection of *their* design. At least three complementary strategies can be used to bring this about.

One way to create a bandwagon is to manage consumers' expectations, giving them the impression that a choice has already been made. Palm used this approach to perfection. Much to the dissatisfaction of its parent, US Robotics, which wanted to distribute the

Pilot through as many retail outlets as possible, Palm decided to sell its new product, at least at the outset, through only a handful of national retail chains. Its goal was to create the impression that the product was a huge hit—so much so that there was not enough of it on the shelf! Sure enough, once they were finally shipped in April 1995, the first few thousand Palm Pilots practically flew off the shelves. Stores began to sell out, creating a buzz about the new product. The shortage was reported on Internet bulletin boards by early Pilot fans and the press interpreted it as an indication that the Pilot was a runaway success.

A second way to speed up the process is simply to engineer a merger with a major rival and use that to retire major competing designs. Consider, for example, the case of the U.K. satellite television market. In 1986, the U.K. government gave a fifteen-year franchise for high-powered direct satellite broadcasting to a consortium called British Satellite Broadcasting (BSB). The consortium planned to develop the market at a reasonable pace, selling 400,000 satellite dishes in 1990, two million by 1992, six million by 1995, and ten million by 2001. However, in June 1988, the News Corporation announced the arrival of Sky Television, which planned to broadcast via a medium-powered satellite called Astra. It began broadcasting in February 1989. BSB missed its initial launch date but finally got on the air in April 1990. The two companies offered incompatible systems—the round satellite dishes of one could not receive the signals sent out to the square dishes of the other and vice versa. This incompatibility meant that consumers had to make a choice and the battle raged across several fronts.

From the start, both companies raced to install as many dishes as possible, each keen to create as large an installed base as possible so as to win the consumer confidence game. Price was the major competitive weapon that both used. Both companies started giving dishes away or subsidized their purchase. Needless to say, both companies were losing money. In 1990, Sky was reputedly losing $3 million per week while BSB was losing $10 million per week. Both companies also raced to sign up influential outside parties (such as the press) in an effort to mobilize consumers who were either unwilling to sign on or were waiting for even better deals on their dishes. They also rushed to sign up the rights to Hollywood films.

Needless to say, this kind of competition could not continue in the face of deep losses and widespread waiting by consumers. In November 1990, the two firms agreed to merge—in effect, Sky took over BSB. Those people who watched satellite television in the 1990s in the United Kingdom watched Sky's version of it, using Sky dishes.

A third way to generate a consumer bandwagon is to use alliance strategies. Co-opting rivals or potential entrants by allowing them to manufacture your chosen design through licensing might limit short-term profits but can accelerate the adoption of a common standard or design. This is the strategy that JVC adopted to establish its VCR standard (the VHS) as dominant in this market, defeating in the process the technically superior Betamax standard from Sony. Despite the superiority of Betamax, JVC was quick in forming alliances with other manufacturers, agreeing to OEM deals. As part of this process, it kept its product design fluid and provided extensive manufacturing and marketing support to its allies. By 1984, JVC had more than forty partners and the VHS format conquered the market.

Consider also how alliances and cooperation helped in the DVD format war. Philips along with Sony invented the CD in 1982. In 1994, again jointly with Sony, it launched a new high-density disk format of the same size as a regular CD but with a much higher storage capacity, combined with the ability to support high-resolution video. The following year, Toshiba's introduction of a similar but incompatible technology threatened to trigger a high-density video and data storage format war similar to the Betamax-VHS video war that took place twenty years earlier. However, this time around, a group of hardware and software companies (including Apple, Compaq, Fujitsu, HP, IBM, and Microsoft) teamed up with Hollywood's entertainment industry and refused to support either of the two formats. Instead, they came up with a "perfect" solution by adopting the best elements of the technology from each camp. The end result was the DVD format, announced in November 1995 and backed by all major players in the consumer electronics, IT, and entertainment industries. The first DVD players appeared in late 1996 and Philips was one of the first companies to manufacture such devices. The company also secured a strong patent pool due to its key role in the invention of the CD and the DVD. To produce DVD players, one needs to license a range of patents owned by different companies, including Philips. To speed up the licensing process, Philips was selected as the DVD industry's licensing agent.

The importance of alliance strategies in creating bandwagons is best seen in cases where competitors failed to do so. The sad outcome in the quadraphonic sound market shows this well. Quadraphonic sound was four-channel surround sound designed to liberate long-suffering music lovers from the confines of stereo. It used four speakers to create the illusion that the sound was coming from all around the listener as it would in a concert hall. By all accounts, it was clearly superior to stereo sound. Yet, it had a short and brutish life in the market that lasted only six years (1971–1976).

It all started in 1971 when Columbia Records (CBS) introduced its SQ (or "matrix") system. Its first rival was the (confusingly labeled) QS system, championed by Sansui, but its major competitor turned out to be the CD-4 ("discrete") system that JVC introduced and RCA records supported. The two main systems were incompatible, forcing the consumers to make a choice. Both, however, were superior to stereo, a fact that led Chase Econometrics to predict in 1974: "Quadraphonic sound will eventually replace stereo . . . by the end of the 1980s, this takeover should be almost complete."

Yet, the new system was dead two years later. Instead of cooperating to establish the quad as the dominant design over stereo, the two main competitors engaged in constant fighting, trying to promote one system over the other. For example, the CBS matrix system was described in the press as "a Mickey Mouse approach which only simulates four channel," while RCA's discrete system was called a "spoiler" and "premature." Consumers wisely decided to play it safe and stay with stereo, audio dealers refrained from promoting uncertain systems, and artists refused to record using the new technology. The new system was dead on arrival—although multi-channel surround sound is today becoming dominant thanks to a new product (the DVD).

It is easy to get competitors to appreciate the importance of alliance strategies in winning a dominant design race but difficult to get them to do it. Although the major participants in the DVD format war managed to cooperate back in 1995 in setting a common DVD format, the peace and harmony over a universal DVD format was (predictably) short-lived. As DVD sales started to take off, there was an urgent need to move from the standard prerecorded DVD format to recordable and re-recordable DVDs that allow users to rewrite and edit DVD contents. In the process, three competing recordable DVD standards emerged:

- DVD-R/-RW, developed by Pioneer and released in 1997
- DVD+R/+RW, developed by Philips and Sony and released in 2001
- DVD-RAM, developed by Hitachi, Toshiba, and Matsushita

The DVD-RAM standard was incompatible with commercial DVD players, thus the real battle for supremacy took place between the first two standards. In the early going, the Philips-Sony standard appeared to have the edge, despite being released four years later than its rival. There were two reasons for this: it was supported by a variety of vendors including Dell, Hewlett-Packard, and Thomson; and it was promoted as a faster standard that was more compatible than the Pioneer standard with older DVD players.

However, matters became complicated when the DVD Forum, the official world body of 220 electronics and media companies that sets DVD standards, decided *not* to approve the DVD+R/+RW format of Philips and Sony. Instead, it backed Pioneer's DVD-R/-RW format. Despite this decision, Philips and Sony are not prepared to give up. They claim that their format already has a significant chunk of the DVD market and that it is perceived by consumers as the dominant design. Still, the lack of endorsement by the DVD Forum prompted Sony to become standard-neutral by deciding to produce DVD drives that will support both formats. This leaves Philips as the only strong advocate of the DVD+R/+RW standard.

This state of affairs convinced industry participants that something had to be done if only to support the growth of next-generation DVDs. In 2003, a powerful consortium of consumer electronics rivals including Philips, Sony, Panasonic/Matshushita, Pioneer, and Hitachi announced that they were joining forces to launch a new generation of DVDs. The new product will have a storage capacity five times higher than current discs and allow for playback and recording of films in high-definition format. This new blue laser DVD format (Blu-ray) is expected to replace the current red laser DVD technology by 2005—eight years after the debut of the first red laser DVDs.

Philips's decision to embrace a universal format for new-generation DVDs was probably driven by a reluctance to be involved in a second (and parallel) format war. Other consortium participants probably thought along the same lines. It is thus surprising that despite this change in attitudes, a second and possibly fiercer format war appears to be on the cards. Toshiba and NEC simultaneously announced their own blue laser DVD format that received the support of the DVD Forum in November 2003. Consortium participants have interpreted Toshiba's decision as a strategic move aimed at renegotiating the lucrative royalty revenues on its DVD patents in return for joining the consortium. Given that the DVD industry appears to be unable to police itself, a format war over future generation DVDs is likely to be decided by the entertainment industry, in the same way that Hollywood forced Philips-Sony and Toshiba to agree on a single DVD standard back in 1995.

It is worth noting that getting a consumer bandwagon rolling involves more than cutting prices, signing up heavyweight partners or sponsors, and refraining from rubbishing the opposition. Not only must a consensus among consumers be created, a consensus among producers of complementary goods must also be established. For example, in the early 1980s, despite the best efforts of JVC and Sony, video cassette recorders were still basically a niche product used mainly for making and viewing home films or for time shifting—that is, recording television programs and watching them later. The big market growth came with the arrival of prerecorded tapes and the rise of the video rental store. JVC helped this process along by keeping its standard "open" and so ensuring that most players in this market had a stake in its eventual triumph.

Reducing Customers' Risk

For any consumer bandwagon to emerge, sustained efforts must be made to reduce the customers' risk when they adopt the product. In a sense, all the strategies designed to create bandwagon effects are also strategies for reducing the risk involved in adopting a product. But much more can and should be done to legitimize a new product and encourage consumer adoption.

The best way to highlight the importance of legitimizing a new product is to focus on a situation where it did not occur. A recent and notorious example of a potentially useful technology that has failed (so far) to become established in Europe is genetically modified (GM) food. There is no question that GM food producers understood the need to establish confidence in their new products and have made serious efforts to establish the new technology and the products that embody it in the market. The new products that have been introduced were exhaustively tested with farmers and regulators. Food manufacturers such as Unilever and Nestlé were provided with information and advice on how to use and market the new products, and these firms have wholeheartedly endorsed the GM products.

Yet no real attempt was made to bring end consumers on board. No one attempted to educate the consumers about the wonders of biotechnology, and no one probed consumer attitudes toward foods that embodied the new technology. In fact, consumers showed deep skepticism about products containing GM foods and displayed a number of phobias about what the new technology might do to them and to the environment. Even more distressing, consumers showed skepticism about the views of experts, politicians, and other early enthusiasts for GM food.

Prompted by the deep antipathy of consumers toward GM food products, supermarkets and restaurants made a positive virtue of removing GM products from their shelves or menus. It is now customary for supermarkets to advertise organic foods, which con-sumers see as both "more natural" and healthier than GM foods—and worth paying a price premium for! The upshot is that many restaurants, food firms, and supermarkets now make a virtue of sell-ing "GM free" food products, legitimizing the absence of something that might, in different circumstances, have itself become legit-imized and accepted as part of the natural order of food production and consumption.

Now, compare this horror story with another that had a much happier ending. Imagine life back in the middle of the nineteenth century. Most people lived on or near farms and consumed a steady diet of fresh food. Even urban dwellers were used to purchasing food in an unprocessed form in open markets full of farm products. Under these (rather idyllic) circumstances, it is hard to understand why anyone in their right mind would contemplate consuming something out of a can or a box. After all, food in a tin or box can-not be seen, felt, smelt, tasted, or tested. And yet, by the end of the nineteenth century, plenty of processed foods were available in cans and boxes and processing such food was something of a growth industry.

It's possible to trace how this happened by studying the actions of one of the pioneers of this business, Henry Heinz. He started his career by selling unadulterated horseradish in clear bottles. This was an interesting move: most bottled horseradish sold at the time was apparently of poor quality and was sold in green or brown bottles, presumably to make it difficult to spot just how poor the product was. Heinz cultivated local grocers and hoteliers and used them to help certify the quality of his product. He managed to associate this reputation with his name, *creating a brand* that helped to facilitate his expansion both geographically and into other products such as celery sauce, pickles, and other condiments. Interestingly, his geographical expansion was into urban areas where resistance to eating anything other than fresh food was low and where housewives often had so many demands on their time that economizing on food preparation time was a priority for them. Similarly, the early products produced by Heinz and other producers did not directly compete with fresh food but were complements to it.

This process of expansion was gradual and occurred in tandem with the complementary activities of other food manufacturers interested in establishing the new business. As other producers expanded into new geographical areas and new products, consumers gradually became more and more used to consuming processed foods that came in cans. Once this happened, it was relatively easy for Heinz to jump into prepared foods (such as baked beans) that competed much more directly with foods that consumers had long been used to purchasing fresh and preparing themselves.

Both examples highlight the importance of developing *customer trust* in a new product. Building a brand can help this process. So can direct communication with the end consumer (rather than the intermediaries) and using credible experts or allies to spread the word. Focusing efforts on consumers that have the lowest resistance level to the new product can also help start a snowball effect, as can using the company's reputation to win early acceptance.

The list of tactics in building customer trust in a new product is endless—just consider how eBay has succeeded in persuading millions of rational human beings to use its service, which is nothing short of miraculous: consumers send their checks to total strangers, knowing full well that they might never receive what they paid for or, even worse, they might pay for a Picasso and end up receiving a schoolchild's scribble! Such things do not happen by accident or luck.

How has eBay managed to build confidence and trust in its service? Enter Pierre Omidyar, the company's founder and current chairman, who started eBay as a hobby in 1995. Omidyar believed that democracy should be the core principle of the company and came up with a brilliant idea, the eBay "feedback forum," through which individuals (suppliers or purchasers) have the opportunity to earn a reputation based on their trading habits. The concept is simple: if we do business together on eBay and if I am happy with the merchandise that you sold me and you are happy with how rapidly I paid you and how I treated you over the e-mail discussion that we had, then we both give good feedback on each other for everyone else to see. This serves to enhance our reputations as users.

The feedback forum is particularly critical for sellers, the vast majority of which are small entrepreneurs who rely on eBay exclusively. Too many negative comments and you are banned as an eBay seller forever. To ensure even higher professional standards among its sellers, eBay has recently announced that it will begin offering low-cost premium health insurance to "Power Sellers," the elite among its legions of private clients. To qualify as a Power Seller, a seller must sell at least $2,000 a month via eBay and achieve 98 percent positive feedback. Not every seller on eBay makes the 98 percent level. In fact, established companies selling on eBay normally fail on this criterion. For example, both IBM and Ritz Camera had positive-feedback levels of only 93 percent. And Disney's feedback was labeled "private," meaning that bidders cannot view comments left by previous buyers. This clearly shows that the huge shipping and handling fees and slow mailing times that big companies can get away with in direct marketing don't work on eBay.

Although eBay relies mainly on buyers and sellers to police themselves, it does investigate fraud claims whenever required to ensure that confidence and trust in its service is maintained at all times. The company is aware that even a handful of unhappy users could damage its reputation. Again, the tactics used by eBay are specific to its industry but the principle is one and the same—to scale up a market, consolidators must invest in reducing the customers' perceived or real risk of adopting the new product.

Building Distribution

Along with investments in advertising and branding, companies that aspire to scale up a new market must also invest heavily to build up distribution sufficient to reach the mass market. Sometimes, this might require setting up a new distribution channel from scratch (as the auto companies had to do at the turn of the century or as Dell did with PCs). But most of the time, what is required is to persuade existing channels to accept the new product. This is more difficult than it sounds. It can be achieved either through the use of market power or through an innovative strategy.

Consider, for example, the experience of Golden Wonder—a Scottish potato chip producer and a division of Imperial Tobacco—in scaling up the potato chip market in the United Kingdom in the 1960s. In the space of ten years (1960–1970), Golden Wonder had increased the size of the market by a factor of six and in the process, increased its market share from almost zero to 40 percent. How did the company do it?

Up until 1960, potato chips were sold mainly to men drinking beer in pubs. The product was sold as a good complement to beer and it was promoted for its thirst-enhancing qualities. Since more than 75 percent of the total sales went through pubs, the main competitors had set up their distribution systems to supply pubs around the country.

Golden Wonder launched its assault in 1961 by promoting potato chips as a nourishing snack food, targeting women and children. Heavy investments in advertising were made to change the image of the product and position it as a snack for domestic consumption. In addition, the company invested heavily in a new production technology to improve the quality of the product, drive down costs, and reduce prices. More important, Golden Wonder developed the distribution channel that was appropriate for its targeted customers—supermarkets and other retail outlets. In the period 1958–1969, turnover of potato chips in pubs went from 75 percent of the total to 25 percent. Turnover in supermarkets and other retail stores went from 25 percent to 65 percent. This was all Golden Wonder's doing—developing the sales force that would go after grocers and giving incentives to independent "merchandising sales cadets" to sell the Golden Wonder product to retailers, arrange for shop displays, and provide point-of-sale promotional material.

Consider, also, the experience of Palm in building up a distribution channel for its organizers. Since it was a division of US Robotics, it first tried to exploit its parent's strong relationships with computer stores. However, the first meeting with Best Buy— a fast-growing mass merchant with more than two hundred stores across the country—made its leaders realize that since they positioned their products as organizers rather than as scaled-down PCs, they had to put them on shelves away from computers. This meant that they also had to develop a different set of contacts among retailers. Early attempts to excite the buyers of organizers in Best Buy also failed—these people wanted more features on the Palm Pilot and could not understand how a $299 organizer could compete with the cheap pocket organizers that were selling at $19.95 at the time. This experience taught Palm that it had to position the product as a PC accessory rather than as an organizer.

It was only when Palm offered to let Circuit City be the exclusive consumer electronics chain to stock Pilot that the first order came in. With Circuit City on board, Palm was able to sign up other retailers, including the computer chains CompUSA and Computer City. After restricting distribution to these few retail outlets to create stock-outs and a buzz about the product, Palm moved on to phase two of its distribution plan shortly after the launch of the product. By signing up Office Depot, Office Max, and Staples, it increased the number of stores carrying Pilots from two thousand to five thousand. By December 1996, Palm had 70 percent of the market.

Building up the distribution to reach the mass market is not cheap. What makes it even more costly is the fact that when a market is scaling up, it actually explodes in size. After years of limited sales, there is a short period when the buying becomes frenzied and sales of the product skyrocket. This means that not only must the necessary distribution be put in place, this has to happen *quickly*. Any sale lost at this stage because the distribution is not in place will go to a competitor. This may mean a customer lost for life. Companies aspiring to scale up a market must be willing to invest a lot of financial and managerial resources in setting up the necessary distribution quickly. To do so, alliance strategies can be very effective.

Supporting Growth of Complementary Goods

Many goods and services are consumed along with other goods and services. Indeed, some products have no value in the absence of such complements. Having a gas-burning car is not of much use if there are no gas stations; CDs are next to useless without a CD player and a set of speakers; a VCR will be an expensive toy without Hollywood movies and video rental shops; and the Microsoft Windows OS will be of little use without a host of compatible software packages.

If that is the case, a company that aspires to scale up its market must find ways to encourage the growth of any products complementary to its own. This is exactly what JVC did in its battle against Sony in the VCR market. By keeping its design open and encouraging other OEMs to produce it, JVC quickly established a large customer base with its VCRs. This, in turn, removed any uncertainty on the part of producers of complementary goods (such as Hollywood studios) as to which format would become dominant and encouraged them to start producing videos in that format. This led to the emergence of video rental shops, and the VCR market simply took off—with the JVC format as the dominant player.

Maintaining a proprietary hold on a design is almost certainly more profitable if that design emerges as the dominant one—something that shareholders in Microsoft know—but the effort can lower the probability of that design winning. By contrast, letting the design become open makes it more likely that the design will become dominant but lowers the profits that the company might gain from such a strategy.

Keeping the standard open is, obviously, only one of the strategies that a company could use to promote the growth of complementary goods. Other strategies might be to provide financial support to producers of complementary products, to develop the complementary goods on its own, to sponsor industry-wide standards, and to use alliances with providers of complementary goods to control key inputs or ensure the provision of the complementary goods. At the end of the day, it is the responsibility of consolidators to promote the growth of complementary goods. Without them, a market cannot be scaled up.

What Skills Are Needed for Scaling Up a Market?

As a way of summarizing the discussion thus far, here's an overview of the strategies and actions that a firm needs to undertake to scale up a niche market:

1. *Target the average consumers (rather than the early adopters) by emphasizing product attributes with mass appeal.* In particular, emphasize low prices that help grow the market. Support low prices by driving down costs. To do so, build market share quickly so as to enjoy economies of scale and learning benefits.

2. *Win the dominant design race.* This can be achieved by creating bandwagon effects.

3. *Reduce customer risk through branding and communication.* Help build as big a consensus as possible across consumers to broaden the initial installed base and widen the ultimate market.

4. *Build distribution that can serve the mass market.* This may require entirely new channels, but it may be possible to simply co-opt channels that already carry other types of products to the market.

5. *Create alliances with key suppliers and producers of complementary goods.* This will ensure the supply of complementary goods and help control access to them.

Now consider two questions: first, What skills or assets are needed to achieve all this? And second, What kind of firms have these skills?

The answer to the first question is straightforward. Creating a dominant design and consolidating a market around it requires the ability to produce a low-cost product at a consistent quality that can be delivered to a large customer base on time and without hassles. This necessitates heavy investments in manufacturing, distribution, and logistics, as well as the ability to build brands and communicate effectively to customers. It also requires efficient inventory and logistics, along with a strong after-sales service organization. Furthermore, a consolidator needs to have strong marketing skills to sway consumers and create the kind of consensus that would support the proposed dominant design. It needs to be able to identify and then reach out to the many potential consumers who are ready to purchase the new product but are unwilling to shoulder the risk of choosing among the many prototypes that first appear on the market. For this, it needs to use its reputation and existing market power to engender trust among consumers.

Creating an organization that can serve a large and rapidly growing market is another set of skills that consolidators need. They require well-thought-out systems and operating controls that keep a tight lid on costs while collecting and exploiting valuable customer information to drive further marketing efforts. They also need processes and cultures that promote efficiency and manufacturing excellence, often at the expense of experimentation and flexibility. Assembling this list of skills is a formidable undertaking. Most of the investments that are required involve substantial sunk costs and should not be undertaken lightly.

What firms can claim that they have the necessary financial resources, the market power and reputation needed, the brand-building skills, and the manufacturing and marketing infrastructure to achieve this? The answer should be obvious: it is the big, established companies that have all these skills and competences. In other words, those companies that we have come to call bureaucratic dinosaurs are the ones that are perfectly positioned to take a niche market and scale it up into a mass market!

What Does This Imply?

Established firms have the skills and competences that allow them to excel in what is really the key in conquering new-to-the-world markets: taking an early market out of the hands of the pioneers and scaling it up into a mass market. This is as innovative as creating the new market in the first place and is the area where established companies can create huge value for themselves. As a final demonstration of what we are arguing, consider how Dell is attempting to grow by moving into the digital music business.

The $35 billion music business is still at the early stages of a transition from CDs to digital downloads, while the portable MP3 player market continues to grow (it is expected to reach $2.6 billion by 2005, up from $1 billion in 2003). In April 2003, Apple Computer, in a masterstroke of technological and marketing acumen, appeared to have seized the initiative in the digital music industry. Apple CEO Steve Jobs pronounced a new era for digital music consumption when he unveiled ultra-thin versions of Apple's already popular iPod portable MP3 player and a long-awaited Internet music store, iTunes.

The iPod was originally launched in 2001, the same year that Napster, the Web site that allowed people to download songs at no cost from other PCs connected to the Internet, was shut down following piracy accusations. Despite its demise, Napster truly popularized the concept of digital music and led to the rapid growth of the portable MP3 player market, in which the iPod is currently the market leader in terms of sales (in August 2003, 18 percent of all digital music players sold in the United States were iPods). Apple's launch of iTunes, which allows users to download songs at 99 cents each and transfer them freely to the new and slimmer version of the iPod, was seen by industry observers as a major step toward complete domination of the digital music industry; no other company could offer such a complete package for digital music lovers. Apple's desire for complete supremacy was exemplified by a very expensive marketing campaign. More than 10 million songs were sold in the first four months following the launch of iTunes, while the new and slimmer iPod looked set to completely dominate the portable MP3 player market.

However, more recent developments suggest a bleaker future for Apple—with the real threat that it might have to settle for only the high-end niche of the market it has pioneered. This is because a host of new rivals have appeared on the horizon. None is more formidable than Dell. On October 28, 2003, Dell unveiled its new Dell DJ MP3 player. The DJ has three distinct advantages over the iPod:

- *It is much cheaper.* The 15GB DJ sells for only $249 (38 percent less than the 15GB iPod, which costs $399) and offers all the key features of its more expensive and glamorous rival. Most important, the Dell DJ can store up to 3,700 songs, which is much more than what most music lovers need.

- *It has a bigger music store.* Dell has teamed up with digital music software firm Musicmatch to power the Dell Music Store. At 99 cents per song downloaded, the Dell Music Store costs exactly the same as iTunes but offers more choice of songs. This is because Musicmatch has licensing deals with thirty independent music companies in addition to the five major record labels, enabling it to offer a much bigger library of tracks (currently more than 250,000, with plans to increase to more than 500,000 by the end of the year). Apple's iTunes was launched with only 200,000 tracks from the five major labels.

- *It works with Windows-based systems.* Dell's DJ can be easily linked to a PC to download songs from the Musicmatch site. This is made possible by the fact that Musicmatch's store is the first Windows-based service in the United States to have a music store built directly into the Jukebox software used to play the music and thus easily accessed by millions of PC users.

Apple's iTunes service does offer a bundling feature, but it was originally designed for Mac users. Although the company recently announced a Windows version of iTunes (ironically by bundling Musicmatch's Jukebox software with Apple's iPod), there is a big question mark as to whether Apple will be able to win over Windows users in the long term. This is made more difficult by the fact that Microsoft insists that Apple has not licensed its Windows Media Technology or its copyright protection software (both of which are used by many of the new iTunes-like services popping up), which means that people who want to access the likes of Musicmatch, Napster 2.0 (Napster's successor), or BuyMusic.com (which offers 79-cent downloads) will not be able to use iPods.

Thus, although it is still early days, it looks possible that Dell may succeed in truly scaling up and ultimately dominating the MP3 player market. The low price of the DJ should enable it to gain market share quickly, and if Apple is unable to match Dell's price, the DJ may soon replace the iPod as the dominant design in consumers' minds. Furthermore, Dell, via its strategic alliance with Musicmatch that allows it to reach many more end users than Apple, seems to be well positioned to create a bandwagon effect that will enhance the DJ's prospects of emerging as the dominant design. As for Apple, although it may still benefit from a further scaling up of the MP3 player market, it will find it very difficult to increase its market share unless it can cut its costs and devise an appropriate strategy to consistently target the mass market of Windows users. The way things stand, it seems highly unlikely it will succeed.

Again, notice that Dell did not create this market, but it is positioning itself to capture most of the value out of its potential growth into a mass market. It would be foolish to argue that scaling up the market is not innovative or value creating. It clearly is and it's also the area where established firms have an advantage over early movers and pioneers because they happen to have the requisite skills and competences to convert niche markets into mass markets. This, therefore, is the area that big, established companies should focus on. This is how they could innovate.

Final Thoughts

In this chapter, we have described how a firm can scale up a market. Of course, the established firms do not have to do all this by themselves—they could acquire the pioneers or license their product designs and technology or even do a joint venture with them. Once they acquire the necessary technology or product design, they can then put their existing skills to work so as to scale up the market. Even though these are viable options for established firms, introducing their own version of the product is probably the best strategy for at least two reasons: first, it is bound to be simpler than acquisition, joint venturing, or licensing, and second, they can design their product in a way that makes it easier and cheaper to scale up. Keep in mind that scaling up is partly about getting the product design right—that is, designing a product in such a way that economies of scale can be exploited. It is likely to be the case that the inventors' original design gives less weight to these factors and more to being a gee-whiz, super-tech product.

Whatever option they use to acquire the necessary product design and technology, established firms must focus their attention on the scaling-up half of innovation. Scaling up a market is an important activity that requires creativity and further innovation.

It is also the area where established firms have an advantage over early movers and pioneers because they happen to have the requisite skills and competences to convert niche markets into mass markets. This, therefore, should be the area that they focus on.

It is important to emphasize that the things that consolidators do—such as entering at the right time, standardizing the product, cutting prices, scaling up production, creating distribution networks, segmenting the market, spending huge amounts of money on advertising and marketing—are exactly the kinds of things that create what we (somewhat inaccurately) call "first-mover advantages." By doing these things, consolidators create buyer loyalty, get preemptive control of scarce assets, go down the learning curve, create brands and reputation, and enjoy economies of scale—all of which give them the advantage versus potential new entrants. Thus, even though pioneers are chronologically first into the market, consolidators are the *real* first movers—they are the first to the market that counts: the mass market!

Chapter Six

Racing to Be Second:
When to Enter New Markets

For many managers, the ability to move fast and to arrive in a new market first is a prized competitive ability. Aside from the sheer joy of winning, this fascination with speed of movement seems to be based on the notion that being first into a new market gives a firm an unassailable advantage over latecomers. Conversely, failure to win the so-called race to market means being condemned forever to the role of fringe follower or me-too player in the market. Consider, for example, the following advice from one of the titans of the technology world, Andrew Grove of Intel:[1] "Opportunity knocks when a technology break or other fundamental change comes your way. Grab it. The first mover and only the first mover, the company that acts while others dither, has a true opportunity to gain time over its competitors—and time advantage, in this business, is the surest way to gain market share."

This is an interesting idea and academics have found it to be valid under certain circumstances, especially for incremental product introductions and the introduction of new brands. However, as we have shown earlier in this book, it is not valid *in the case of radically new markets*.

When a new technological trajectory opens up new market possibilities, everyone familiar with the new technology has a choice to make. Should they try to enter first with what they think might be a winning product, or should they wait to see what happens? Those who choose to move first—we have called them colonizers—are the trailblazers who explore the technology and educate at least some potential users to its delights. They therefore begin the process of establishing the new market. But as we have seen, most firms that take this option exit the market pretty much as fast as they enter. This is not to say that their presence in the market is not profitable—often it is very profitable, but on a scale appropriate to the market at the time that they are in it.

The firms that end up capturing the new market—we have called them consolidators—are those firms that time their entry into the market so they appear just when the dominant design is about to emerge. In this chapter, we will call this a *fast-second* strategy and propose that for big, established firms contemplating entry into a new radical market, this is the best strategy to follow. Needless to say, timing one's entry to coincide with the emergence of the dominant design is not the only thing required for a firm to conquer the new market. As we showed in Chapter Five, consolidators have to proactively and strategically invest to grow the market and capture the mass consumer. Often this requires heavy investments in exploiting scale economies, cutting costs and prices, developing strong brands, and controlling the channels of distribution to the mass market. But a prerequisite for all this is correct timing of entry.

A fast-second strategy differs from both a first-mover and (more important) a second-mover strategy. A first-mover strategy would involve getting into the market quickly and producing your own product variants, hoping that your product emerges as the dominant design. A second-mover strategy would involve waiting for the dominant design to be completely established and accepted in the market and then producing a me-too product under that standard. A fast-second strategy would involve waiting for the dominant design to begin to emerge and then moving in to *be part of that* (that is, helping to create it).

Everyone knows what the second-mover strategy involves— competing on costs and low prices and trying to be *better* than the competition. But what does one have to do to be a successful fast-second player? This is a strategy that IBM made famous in mainframes but others have followed successfully as well: GE in CT scanners, JVC in video recorders, Canon in cameras, Black & Decker in food processors, P&G in diapers, Sharp in fax machines, and Texas Instruments in pocket calculators. How then could a firm run a race knowing full well before and during the race that its goal is (or should be) not to win but to finish second, right behind the early runner?

We explore these questions in this chapter. Timing is a key element of competitive strategy but timing is more than just running as fast as you can. By drawing a distinction between first-mover, fast-second, and imitative second-mover strategies, we aim to make the following points:

- First movers are rarely able to capture much in the way of first-mover advantages in radically new markets. This is often the case because a market has to be large and relatively settled for first-mover advantages to exist and very young radical markets are typically neither large nor settled.

- Second movers who wait until a dominant design emerges to enter the market have to face formidable and entrenched competitors. To succeed, they must either compete on price or find ways to break the rules of the game in the industry.

- Fast-second movers do not wait until the dominant design emerges. They time their entry to coincide with the emergence of the dominant design and they actively influence which design will emerge the winner.

- The optimal strategy for established firms contemplating entry into a new radical market is fast-second entry. By moving at the right time and by helping develop the mass market, these firms create the so-called first-mover advantages.

Moving Second

When a radically new market arrives on the scene, it doesn't make sense to rush into it. Contrary to prevailing beliefs, first movers into radically new markets rarely survive the consolidation of the market—most disappear, never to be heard from again. Despite all the evidence pointing to this fact, most of us still believe in first-mover advantages and the beauty of pioneering! The problem is that the pioneers of new-to-the-world markets die quickly and without first growing the market to a size respectable enough to win them attention. As a result, they quickly vanish from people's memories and the glory that in truth belongs to them is thrust upon those who came after them and successfully scaled the market up into a mass market.

Clearly then, the optimal strategy is to try to avoid moving first into radically new markets and attempt to enter second. However, second movers still have quite a wide range of choice about when exactly to act. There are a variety of ways in which one can come second in a race, and it is important to understand that several quite different second-mover strategies are available to firms who choose not to move first (or who have not been able to do so). It is worth distinguishing at least two generic types of second mover.

The first generic type of second mover is a *fast-second* mover. These are firms that arrive in the market very soon after the first mover, so soon in fact that they do not allow the first mover to build up much of a competitive advantage. How big a window of opportunity is open to second movers depends on just how quick first movers are to take advantage of being first.

Fast-second movers are often established firms whose business is threatened by the new technology. It is not in their interest for the new technology to become established, but once it seems likely that the new technology will take hold, it is in their interest to become leaders in the new market. Hence they have little incentive to move first but every incentive to move fast when someone else does.

Fast-second strategies are more than a fancy description of doing nothing. They are, in fact, very active. A fast-second mover has to be as ready to move as any first mover—it must have mastered the new technology and must have a product design, a set of manufacturing and distribution plans, and a marketing strategy in place. In fact, it must do everything that a first mover does, and more: it must wait until someone else moves.

This is a strategy that IBM made famous in the days of main-frames. The early pioneers of mainframes were various government agencies. Although companies like IBM were aware of the challenge to their existing businesses, they were slow to move in the market. IBM supported the development of particular machines in 1939 and again in 1945, mostly as a strategy of keeping in touch with the market. The first commercial computer, UNIVAC, had the market to itself until 1953, when IBM introduced its first business computers. IBM did not aspire to technological dominance but relied instead on its sales force and its close knowledge of, and association with, business users. In late 1954, UNIVAC had an installed base that was eight times larger than IBM's. Just six years later, this market share ratio had reversed, with IBM emerging as the leader. Most of the rest of the history of the mainframe business followed the same pattern: IBM rarely pioneered the new generation of mainframes that came to market but always came in a fast second, using this strategy to gain control of the market. IBM applied much the same strategy for its entry into the personal computer market.

The second generic type of second mover is the *imitative* entrant. Imitative entry is a slow-second strategy that offers little in the way of innovation to the market. It is designed not so much to take advantage of new technological possibilities as to capitalize on the market opportunities created by earlier movers in a market opened up by new technology. Imitative entrants almost always sell on low prices. Sometimes they leverage a valuable brand or control over retail outlets. In part, they do so because they are free riders—they are taking advantage of market opportunities created by others, minimizing the costs of setting up and creating a new product. But they are also low-price players in part because they have to be: to attract customers away from first movers they need to have something to offer. If it is not a new product with new product attributes then it almost certainly has to be an established product at a low price.

Virgin is a classic imitative entrant, but with a slight twist. It has entered numerous apparently unconnected markets—record production and retailing, train services, airlines, cosmetics, financial services, and mobile telephony, to name just a few—without being first in any case. What Virgin brings to the table is a reasonably well-known brand. The firm obviously believes that the value of this brand is big enough to allow it to compete in all these markets without having to resort to low prices. It does undercut incumbents in its chosen markets but not by much. It also fails far more often than it succeeds, but since imitative entry is typically inexpensive (at least relative to first or fast-second strategies), this high failure rate has apparently not seriously undermined the profitability of the group.

Like fast-second entry, imitative entry is not a fancy way of doing nothing. Imitative entrants are always active, always on the lookout for an edge, whether that is a market niche that nobody is serving, a lower cost base, or a valuable brand that might be extended into yet another market. What they do not do, however, is compete head to head with first movers—they do not typically try to displace the leader or introduce a new dominant design; instead, they try to live with the leader and survive. They do not usually challenge the rules of the competitive game in the market—they just try to play that game a little better than anyone else.

Fast-Second Strategies

The key to a fast-second strategy is timing, and in new markets this is very difficult to get right. The turning point in the development of a radical new market is the emergence of a dominant design. Therefore, playing the fast-second game is all about introducing what effectively becomes the dominant design in that market. This, in turn, requires understanding just when the market is ready to adopt a dominant design. But how does one know when this is going to happen?

This task is especially complicated in new markets because new product development is continuous and takes place in real time. As new entrants come into the market bringing with them their own product variants, learning takes place. On the supply side of the market, the introduction of different product variants and production processes allows producers to understand and then explore the limits of the new technology. Producers need to understand how to make the new products that they have designed and how to design a product that can be produced economically. On the demand side, consumers need to learn about the new product and how to use it best. They also need to understand which product attributes are most important and how to fit the new product into their lifestyles. As learning takes place, new and improved product variants continually appear in the market.

All this suggests that predicting which of the many product variants that come and go will eventually emerge as the dominant design is a difficult and complex task. Consider, for example, the case of the computer operating system (OS). There is now a single dominant OS design for personal computers and that is Microsoft Windows. This was not the first OS in the market. CP/M was the first on the market, adapted from a system used on DEC's minicomputers. It prospered as the market for personal computers gradually expanded. As CP/M established itself, applications writers began writing software to work with it. Among these early applications writers was a young firm called Microsoft.

Despite CP/M's early lead, its position was more precarious than it seemed at the time. Operating systems must bear a one-to-one relationship with computer chips, and since the market for personal computers had not yet consolidated, it was not clear which computer chip would emerge as the standard and whether CP/M would be the one to establish a one-to-one relationship with that chip manufacturer. In fact, Microsoft wrote the operating system MS-DOS for the IBM personal computer—or more accurately, adapted an existing operating system that it bought from a small firm called Seattle Computer Products. The establishment of the IBM personal computer and the emergence of Intel's chips as the industry standard brought MS-DOS to the fore and accelerated the demise of CP/M.

The next big step in operating systems was the development of the graphical user interface, something that Microsoft Windows has made us all familiar with. This was developed in a number of laboratories, most notably Xerox's PARC facility in Silicon Valley. It was featured in the Xerox Star that was introduced in 1981, and Apple also introduced it in its (failed) Lisa computer. Windows was a rather late entrant, but it emerged dominant when it finally came to market in 1985. In part, its success was based on its compatibility with MS-DOS—they were bundled together—which made it less threatening to MS-DOS users. It was also relatively inexpensive, worked relatively well, and—more important—was hooked into the personal computer that had emerged as the industry standard.

This process of real-time new product development is the key to the early development of the market. But it is extremely difficult to predict where it will go and how long it will take to get there. All this means that guessing just when the market is ready for a dominant design is not straightforward. There are, however, a number of pointers that might be used, including the following:

- A *slowing in the rate of innovation:* The experimentation process involves bringing products with new attributes and new architectures to market. There are, however, only just so many new ways of doing the same old thing and at some point it will become clear that new product variants are less radical and involve less in the way of new features than before, suggesting that the new technology has been fairly fully explored and is relatively mature.

- A *growing sense of legitimacy:* As consumers become more and more familiar with the new product—more used to what it can do and more disposed to believe that it is worth having— it gradually becomes more accepted. Early enthusiasts are not the important consumers in this. Rather, it is the great majority of consumers who will form the basis of the mass market that matter. When they have come to accept that the new product exists and is potentially useful for them, the market is ready to take off.

- *Appearance of complementary goods producers:* All goods are consumed as part of a bundle of complementary products, and firms that are in complementary product markets are likely to be interested in the future of the new product. Since the design of complementary goods depends on the dominant design, these firms have a real interest in which design prevails in the new market. As interested and intelligent players, such firms are likely to be particularly good sources of information about what is happening.

Fast-second movers do not simply wait until the dominant design emerges—they actively take part in creating it. The important point is that dominant designs do not emerge from markets—they are imposed on markets by would-be champions. Whether a particular dominant design is right for a market depends on how the champion of that design brings it to market and what it does with it when it gets there. As noted in Chapter Five, these are the kinds of tactics associated with the successful imposition of a dominant design on a market:

- *Pricing:* To establish dominance in the market, a design needs to command a fairly wide consensus among consumers. One easy basis for achieving such a consensus is through low prices. Hence, a firm intent on establishing a dominant design will invest in achieving economies of scale, going down a learning curve, or both.
- *Target market:* A firm interested in establishing a dominant design needs to create a bandwagon. The easiest way to do this is to get early consumers to recruit further consumers through word-of-mouth, sharing their experience and enthusiasm. Hence, the choice of an initial target market is an important key to success.

- *Distribution:* It is one thing to have a target market—both initially and in the long run—and it is quite another to get access to that market. To establish a new product in a mass market a firm needs to make the product easily available to consumers. To the extent that consumers trust particular retailers, getting the product into those retailers' outlets is part of the strategy of gaining acceptance for the new product design.

- *Alliance strategy:* Part of the trick of establishing a particular product as a dominant design is reducing the competition from other designs. As we have seen, young markets are full of firms—most of which know that very few are going to survive in the long run. A firm that loses out in the race to establish a dominant design faces exit, or, if it is lucky, a tenuous life in a market niche somewhere. Competitor firms that do not expect to survive are often quite happy to ensure their place in the market by joining the dominant design and producing variants of it. Not only does such an alliance strategy reduce the number of competing designs but it can create the sense that a choice has already been made.

- *Confidence:* At the end of the day, establishing a dominant design or a standard is a matter of psyching out the opposition. Whenever network effects appear, whenever complementary goods producers must wait until a design is established before they can enter the market, and whenever consumers are afraid of being orphaned with obsolete products, the optimal strategy of such players is to wait and see what happens. A firm that wishes to capture them must persuade them that a choice has been made, that the dominant design has actually emerged, and that the competition for the market is all over save for the shouting.

The Spoils of Capturing the Mass Market

The champion whose product forms the basis of the dominant design often develops substantial and very long-lived first-mover advantages from being the product champion. Notice, however, that most of these so-called first movers were not, in fact, the first into the market. All of them were preceded by many entrepreneurial start-ups, now forgotten, whose work formed the foundation upon which these rather later entrants built. These first movers were first only in the sense that they were the first to champion the particular product variant that became the dominant design. They were first when the mass market emerged (not when the product emerged), and this, of course, is why they ended up with most of the profits.

What kind of first-mover advantages accrue to these fast-second movers who capture the mass market? First movers into a market gain advantages not so much by being first as by what they do in the market when they are first. Essentially, first-mover advantages arise whenever a first mover can alter competitive conditions in a market in such a way as to disadvantage later entrants. This happens whenever it can put obstacles in the way of entrants that limit their penetration into the market without too much of a sacrifice in profits on the first entrant's part. Economists call such obstacles *barriers to entry*. Expressed as simply as possible, gaining advantage from first movement is basically about creating barriers to entry. Barriers arise on both the demand and the supply side of the market.

A first mover that can lock in consumers to its product effectively shrinks the market available to later-moving firms. Lock-in is a matter of degree and is usually expressed in terms of *switching costs*: the higher the switching costs, the larger the price premium that a firm can charge without losing its customers to an undercutting rival. When switching costs are so high that an undercutting firm cannot attract customers without suffering losses, then those customers are truly locked in to the first mover. High switching costs clearly reduce the prospects of entry: a later entrant has to either manage with fewer potential customers or cut prices far enough to attract those the first mover has locked in.

Switching costs can be created in many ways. When consumers first buy a very new good, their choice is as much an investment decision as a consumption decision. Having made a choice and having invested in understanding the product of their choice, they may well be reluctant to continue to experiment by trying other products (unless, of course, they are unhappy with their first choice). For *experience goods*, which need to be consumed before they can be fully valued, such investments are risky and consumers who are happy with the product they are currently consuming will need clear incentives to continue experimenting.

Switching costs can also be created by the provision of complementary goods: many goods are consumed in bundles and whenever the consumption of a particular good (like a CD) requires a complementary good (like a CD player), the prior choice of complementary good rules out certain subsequent choices (in this case, using digital audio tapes or even old-fashioned LPs to play music). Hence a first mover that follows a strategy of facilitating the provision of complementary goods that complement its product but not those of its rivals is effectively raising switching costs. Switching costs might also just be a matter of recognition or familiarity: an established product that is widely known and trusted is, somehow, different from a new upstart that no one has ever heard of—something normally referred to by saying that the established firm has a brand that consumers value.

Finally, some switching costs are collective and arise from so-called *network effects*, which appear when the consumption of a good depends on the number of other people all using the same good. For example, if you are the only one in the world with a fax machine, you possess a useless device—you have no one to send faxes to or receive them from. Similarly, if you are the only person in your neighborhood with a Betamax video cassette recorder, you will not be able to swap tapes with the neighbors (who are all using VHS video cassette recorders), and it is unlikely that your local video rental shop will include many shelves of Betamax cassettes just for you. Moreover, the more people your network includes, the larger and more impressive the video rental shop is likely to be. Collective switching costs are a major obstacle for entrants because they require that every consumer must switch to the same alternative product if network effects are to be preserved, and this can be very difficult to manage. What is worse, none of the consumers will want to switch without being sure that everyone else will do so too, a chicken-and-egg problem if there ever was one.

The famous example of inertia created by network effects is the QWERTY keyboard. First developed in the days when typewriters were strictly mechanical, the QWERTY keyboard was designed to prevent the type bars from jamming. The basic design principle was to separate frequently used letters. A more natural arrangement, one would have thought, would be to put frequently used letters in the middle of the keyboard where all the action is. Since the jamming problem has not been an issue for perhaps a hundred years (electric typewriters had no type bars and neither do personal computers), one would have thought that something a bit more ergonomically sensible might have displaced QWERTY by now. And yet, just which firm is going to be interested in pioneering a new keyboard? This would involve converting millions of touch-typing and hunt-and-peck QWERTY users and just how interested are any of them in learning the layout of a new computer keyboard?

First-mover advantages can also arise on the supply side of the market. Early movers are often able to buy or gain control of key assets (such as key intellectual property rights and scarce retail shelf space) or key inputs (such as very highly specialized workers and necessary natural resources). Furthermore, they often get a head start in moving down the learning curve or in building the facilities necessary to take advantage of economies of scale. One way or another, seizing such opportunities is likely to create a cost advantage for the leader that will make it difficult for later-moving entrants to establish themselves in the market (particularly if they are following a me-too imitative strategy).

It is worth making one final point about first-mover advantages, namely that the list of things that create first-mover advantages is suspiciously similar to the list of things that a consolidator needs to do to grow the market (see Chapter Five). Although it is clearly a smart strategy for a first mover to come into the market and try to increase customer switching costs or create a cost advantage vis-à-vis later rivals, the plain fact is that such advantages are often a happy by-product of the normal actions that a firm must take if it is to kick-start a new market. As noted, making a new product attractive to the mass market requires low prices, complementary goods, and customer network effects. Markets do not usually take off and become large until prices have fallen, network effects are available, and complementary goods have been provided. A first mover who is able to do all of this not only helps develop the market but also gains access to a number of possible first-mover advantages.

The Costs of Being Second

Moving "first" makes it possible in principle for a smart firm to gain a number of advantages over its later-arriving rivals. However, first movement is both costly and risky, and it is possible that the costs of moving first are not always worth these benefits. In particular, a first mover incurs three types of costs.

The first is the cost of creating a new market. As noted, new markets require infrastructures and at least some consumers need to be alerted to what the new product offers and be persuaded to buy. Complementary goods producers need to be encouraged to enter the action, scarce resources and specialized inputs need to be located or created, and provision must be made for consumers to realize any network effects that will be available. A bandwagon must be started to draw new consumers into the market and this means (among other things) launching the product into the right market segment in the first place. Even if many of these activities do not require much in the way of cash, they may require new skills and competencies. They may also be time intensive and, therefore, carry a large opportunity cost.

The second cost is that associated with risk. Three risks are typically involved in setting up a new market: the risk that the technology will not, after all, deliver what is promised; the risk that there will not be enough of a market for the products of that technology; and the risk of being preempted by another firm (or being driven from the market by an established firm whose business is threatened by the new market). Needless to say, technological and market risks are highest in supply-push innovation processes that push up new technologies in a raw and relatively undigested form without the guidance of well-formed demand. Of these three risks, the first two are particularly high for a first mover. However, a first mover that gets to market and gets established is able to avoid the third risk.

The third cost is slightly more subtle. It is almost always the case that there is a *time-cost* trade-off in the development of new technologies, meaning that the faster the development time, the more costly it is. Time-cost trade-offs arise because rush projects are always inefficient: too many resources are thrown at a project too fast, very little time is allowed for reflection, and the assembly and deployment of research inputs is not particularly economical. Firms anxious to be first to the market are quite likely to incur much bigger development costs than firms who attempt to do much the same thing but in less of a hurry. Indeed, firms that move too quickly are more likely to fail to reach their target than slower, more reflective movers who look before they leap.

The IBM personal computer is a classic example of just how the costs of first movement can be avoided without necessarily sacrificing first-mover advantages. Arguably, the first personal computer was the Altair 8800, introduced in 1975. The Altair was actually just a kit—you had to build it yourself—and the main users were computer hobbyists who had as much interest in building personal computers as in using them. The Altair did not last long and was soon pushed out of the market by Radio Shack and Apple, firms that headed a lengthy list of early entrants into this market.

Both IBM and Xerox had flirted with this market—the long-forgotten IBM 5100 introduced in 1975 was only twenty times the cost of the Altair and had a minuscule screen. However, after further waiting and watching, IBM introduced the IBM PC late in 1981. It was not state-of-the-art and used off-the-shelf parts and software written by a small and obscure Seattle software house, but it instantly became the standard in the market. In 1982, about 150 companies produced personal computers in the United States, but the IBM PC led to a fearsome shakeout. Its access to customers, brand name, and ability to exploit scale economies, plus the general expectation that IBM was bound to be among the survivors, ensured that when the dust settled, IBM and its personal computer led the market.

The IBM personal computer story contains a further twist. What IBM seems to have gotten right was the timing of its entry into the market. Consumers were ready for personal computers and the IBM personal computer matched the needs of those consumers at a decent price. However, IBM failed to spot just how quickly the market was going to take off. In addition, the general standard set by the IBM personal computer made it easy for clones to enter and produce IBM-compatible machines. IBM apparently thought that it could protect its market because of its market power and brand and by moving down the learning curve fast enough to be safe from clones. It also hoped that protection would come by controlling a key bit of technology (the ROM-BIOS, which, as it happened, Compaq reverse engineered in record time). As we all know, all these proved to be false hopes.

Moving Too Slow

It is worth emphasizing that fast-second strategies are not risk free. The early history of most markets is littered with the corpses of firms that tried and failed to impose a particular dominant design on the market. Even larger is the list of firms whose fast-second strategy was just too slow, leaving them competing for a place in a market that had already been defined by another firm. In such cases, the only strategy that latecomers can adopt against entrenched first movers is to strategically innovate by breaking the rules of the game in the market.

Breaking the Rules

Existing academic evidence shows that entering a market after it has been established (and in the process attacking entrenched competitors) often ends up in failure.[2] Several studies have found that on average, the probability that the top-ranked firm in a particular industry will survive as number one is above 95 percent—an almost certainty. For the second-ranked firm, the probability of survival is about 90 percent, and for the third-ranked firm, it is 80 percent. In fact, most of the turnover that occurs among the top five in an industry is because of mergers rather than displacement by new entrants.

Thus, despite some well-documented examples of dramatic success against the industry leader, such as Canon against Xerox and Komatsu against Caterpillar, the truth of the matter is that the vast majority of late entrants fail quite miserably. Nonetheless, firms such as Honda, IKEA, easyJet, and CNN entered established markets and did quite well, despite all the odds against them. How did they do it? The evidence points to a simple answer: latecomers can improve the probability of successful entry in established markets by attacking the entrenched competitors through unorthodox strategies.

The rise and fall of Xerox in the period 1960–1990 highlights this simple but powerful point. In the 1960s, Xerox put a lock on the copier market by following the well-defined and successful strategy illustrated in Exhibit 6.1. The main elements of this strategy were the following: Having segmented the market by volume, Xerox decided to go after the corporate reproduction market by concentrating on copiers designed for high-speed, high-volume needs. This inevitably defined Xerox's customers as big corporations, which in turn determined its distribution method: the direct sales force. At the same time, Xerox decided to lease rather than sell its machines, a strategic choice that had worked well in the company's earlier battles with 3M.

The Xerox strategy was clear and precise, with well-defined and sharp boundaries. Critical choices were made as to what kind of customers to target (big corporations); what product features to emphasize (high speed); and what activities to perform (direct sales force and leasing). These were not easy choices to make and there must have been lively debates and disagreements within Xerox on whether the choices were the correct ones. Yet, at the end of the day, decisions were taken and hard choices made. At the time they

Exhibit 6.1. Xerox Versus Canon:
A Case of Different Strategies.

Strategy Component	Xerox	Canon
Product	Plain paper copiers (PPCs)	Start with coated paper copiers (CPCs) and then move to PPCs
Copier volume	High	Low → High
Targeted customers	Big corporations	End users
Method of selling	Lease	Sell
Distribution	Sales force	Dealer network
Differentiating features	Speed	Quality and price

were good ones. Xerox prospered because it developed a distinctive strategic position in its industry, with well-defined customers and products and focused activities to bring them together. Throughout the 1960s and early 1970s, Xerox maintained a return on equity (ROE) of around 20 percent.

Xerox's strategy proved so successful that several new competitors, among them IBM and Kodak, tried to enter this huge market by basically adopting the same or similar strategies. Fundamentally, their strategy was to grab market share by being *better* than Xerox—by offering better products or better service at lower prices. For example, IBM entered the market in 1970 with its first model, the IBM Copier I, which was clearly addressing the medium- and high-volume segments and was marketed by IBM's sales force on a rental basis. Similarly, Kodak entered the market in 1975 with the Ektaprint 100 copier/duplicator, which was aimed for the high-volume end of the market and was sold as a high-quality but low-price substitute for Xerox.

Neither of these corporate giants managed to make substantial inroads in the copier business. While there are many possible reasons for this failure, their inability to differentiate themselves from Xerox was undoubtedly one of them. Unlike Xerox, both IBM and

Kodak failed to identify or create a distinctive strategic position in the industry. Instead, they tried to invade Xerox's position and fought for market share by trying to become better than Xerox. Given the first-mover advantages that Xerox enjoyed in its own strategic position, it is no surprise that IBM and Kodak failed.

Canon, on the other hand, chose to play the game differently. Having determined in the early 1960s to diversify out of cameras and into copiers, Canon segmented the market by end user and decided to target small and medium-sized businesses while also producing PC copiers for the individual. At the same time, Canon decided to sell its machines through a dealer network rather than lease them, and while Xerox emphasized the speed of its machines, Canon elected to concentrate on quality and price as its differentiating features (also shown in Exhibit 6.1). Cutting the story short, where IBM's and Kodak's assault on the copier market failed, Canon's succeeded: within twenty years of attacking Xerox, Canon emerged as the market leader in volume terms.

Again, there are many reasons behind the success of Canon. Notice, however, that just as Xerox did twenty years before it, Canon also created for itself *a distinctive strategic position* in the industry—a position that was different from Xerox's position: whereas Xerox targeted big corporations as its customers, Canon went after small companies and individuals; whereas Xerox emphasized the speed of its machines, Canon focused on quality and price; and whereas Xerox used a direct sales force to lease its copiers, Canon used its dealer network to sell its copiers. Rather than try to beat Xerox at its own game, Canon triumphed by creating its own unique strategic position that allowed it to attack Xerox through a differentiated strategy.

As with Xerox, these were not the only choices available to Canon and undoubtedly serious debates and disagreements must have taken place within Canon as to whether these were the right choices to pursue. Yet choices were made and a clear strategy with sharp and well-defined boundaries was put in place. Like Xerox,

Canon was successful because it chose a unique and well-defined strategic position in the industry—one with distinctive customers, products, and activities.

The Canon success story contains valuable lessons for all late-comers in a market. Without the benefit of a new technological innovation, it is extremely difficult for any firm to successfully attack the established industry leaders or to successfully enter a market where the dominant design has emerged and the rules of the game have been established. In these situations, significant shifts in market share and company fortunes can take place only if the latecomer introduces a strategy that changes the rules of the game in the industry.

Final Thoughts

Running fast is always a smart strategy whenever the benefits of winning are larger than the costs of doing so. Since running fast is very costly (and tiring), it is important to be sure that there are benefits to be gained by winning and that they can be captured. As we have seen, it is rarely the case that the first movers are able to capture much in the way of so-called first-mover advantages in new markets. In a sense, this is the case because a market has to be large and relatively settled for first-mover advantages to exist and very young markets are typically neither large nor settled.

It is only when the market is ready to become a mass market that first movement matters. The market is ready to become a mass market when a dominant design emerges. It follows, then, that the right strategy to adopt in such markets is what we have called a *fast-second* strategy, entering when it seems likely that the market is ready to accept a dominant design. A fast-second player that establishes a dominant design and scales up the market is, in fact, nothing more than a *consolidator*, to use the language of early chapters. Furthermore, the process by which a fast-second mover attacks a first mover and establishes itself in the market is exactly the same that a consolidator uses to grow and develop a mass market from an initial market niche.

Chapter Seven

The Changing Basis of Competition

The scaling up of a market is associated with a sudden and rapid growth in the number of customers purchasing the new product. This explosive growth has been labeled a *tornado* by some observers and is depicted in marketing textbooks as the famous S-shaped product life cycle curve. This, of course, is not the case for every new product. In fact, most new products never make it beyond the original tiny niche of early pioneers. Many languish in a small niche for years and either fail completely or grow into a specialist part of some bigger market. But a few make it to the promised land!

As noted in Chapter Five, this is not a matter of accident or luck. It takes a concerted effort on the part of a company to successfully scale up a market, and those that succeed in doing so enjoy the fruits of their labor. These are the firms that people mistakenly call first movers. They are not. Forgotten in all of this are the actual first movers—those pioneers that rushed into the new market only to disappear once the dominant design emerged.

As the market goes through an explosive growth phase, the basis of competition shifts. Whereas the early market displayed a very fluid structure with no meaningful distinction between entrants and incumbents, the situation now begins to resemble an established market as we know it, with permanent, long-term residents and well-defined rules of the game. And whereas the early market was characterized by tremendous product variety as well as constant entry and exit and substantial uncertainty, the market now consolidates around a dominant design and loses its revolving-door dynamism.

To prosper in this changing environment, established firms must radically rethink how to compete. In many cases, they will have to unlearn everything that has made them successful so far. In this chapter, we explore the most important changes that need to take place if the company is to succeed in the new market. We aim to make the following points:

- Having scaled up the market, the winning company must realize that it cannot serve everybody in this market. As the market fragments into distinct customer segments, the company must decide which strategic position in the industry it should claim as its own. This requires that difficult choices be made.

- Competition after the emergence of the dominant design comes to focus more and more on price. This means that the sources of competitive advantage lie increasingly with lowering costs.

- The need to reduce costs triggers a number of changes in the industry. The first of these changes is a shift away from product innovation toward *process* innovation.

- As the market matures further, strategic innovation becomes a major source of competitive advantage. Unfortunately, established companies find it hard to pursue this kind of innovation.

- Mature industries go through vertical disintegration of production. The market separates into different components or modules. The efficiency that results from all this is usually accompanied by a reduction in the flexibility of established competitors.

The Need to Make Difficult Choices

Having scaled up the market from a small niche to a mass market and having claimed a leadership position in that market, it is easy to be carried away by success and assume that you can serve the whole market successfully. It is a tempting thought but it is also a thought that leads to disaster! No company can be everything to everybody. Difficult strategic choices must be made, which means that the company will have to select which customers it will *not* serve and which product features it will *not* offer.

This is a hard lesson to learn. After all, the success of the company in scaling up the market was based on selling a standard product to the mass market, focusing on price. Why should this strategy change now that the battle has been won?

The reason is simple. In the early going, when the market takes off, customers are eager to get their hands on the product. They want their first digital camera, or their first handheld computer, or their first mobile phone. They want the *commodity*. The company's focus should be to get the standard product to these customers as quickly and cheaply as possible.

However, as other competitors start serving the growing market, supply catches up with demand. At this stage, customers begin to express their individual preferences—some want a cheap product; others do not mind paying a premium price as long as the product is well-designed; yet others demand bells and whistles on their product. A company cannot serve all of these needs nor can it keep all customers happy. Choices will have to be made. Specifically, the company will have to decide which strategic position in the market to claim as its own and which positions to leave for its competitors.

Staking a Unique Strategic Position

What exactly do we mean when we say that a company must claim a strategic position as its own? Keep in mind that every industry has several viable positions that companies can occupy. The essence of strategy is, therefore, to choose the *one* position that a company will claim as its own. A strategic position is nothing more than the sum of the answers that a company gives to three questions:

- *Who* should I target as customers?
- *What* products or services should I be offering them?
- *How* should I do this in an efficient way?

Strategy is all about making tough choices on these three dimensions: the customers a firm will focus on and the customers it will not, the products it will offer and the ones it will not, the activities it will perform and the ones it will not. These are not easy decisions to make and each question has many possible answers, all of them possible and logical. As a result, these kinds of decisions will unavoidably be preceded by debates, disagreements, politicking, and indecision. Yet at the end of the day, a firm cannot be everything to everybody; clear and explicit decisions must be made. These choices may turn out to be wrong—but that is not an excuse for not deciding!

It is absolutely essential that the company makes clear and explicit choices on these three dimensions because these choices become the parameters within which people are allowed to operate with autonomy. They define for everybody in the organization what is acceptable and what is not—the customers it will not pursue, the investments it will not make and the competitors it will not respond to. Without these clear parameters, the end result can be chaos. Seen another way, it would be foolish and dangerous to allow people to take initiatives without some clear parameters guiding their actions.

The most common source of strategic failure is when companies fail to make clear and explicit choices on these three dimensions. This is a point that several strategy academics have emphasized. Yet it is easy to fall into the trap of not making clear choices because choosing is difficult. At the time of choosing, nobody knows for sure whether a particular idea will work out or if the choices made are really the most appropriate ones. One could reduce the uncertainty at this stage by either evaluating each idea in a rigorous way or by experimenting with the idea in a limited way to see if it works or not. However, it is crucial to understand that uncertainty can be reduced but not eliminated. No matter how much experimentation it carries out and no matter how much thinking its people do, the time will come when the firm must decide one way or another. Choices have to be made and these choices may turn out to be wrong. However, lack of certainty is no excuse for indecision.

Not only must the company make clear choices on these parameters, it must also attempt to make choices that are different from the choices its competitors have made. A company will be successful if it chooses a distinctive or unique (that is, different from competitors) strategic position. Sure, it may be impossible to come up with answers that are 100 percent different from the answers of competitors, but the ambition should be to create as much differentiation as possible.

The Ford Model T Example. It may be worth highlighting all this with an example. The story of the Ford Model T is a very good example of how a product that takes the mass market by storm can quickly become obsolete if the company perseveres with a "one product for all" strategy and fails to pay attention to changing consumer needs as the market matures.

When Henry Ford introduced the Model T in 1908 he promised: "I will build a motor car for the great multitude." And so he did, as Ford's Model T became the world's first modern mass-produced automobile. In the nineteen years of the Model T's existence, it sold fifteen and a half million units in the United States, almost a million in Canada, and a quarter-million in Great Britain, with a production total amounting to half the auto output of the world.

The success of the Model T (famously known as the Tin Lizzie) was inextricably linked to Henry Ford's vision of the car as the ordinary man's utility vehicle. The Model T was not luxurious, but it took people from one place to another cheaply and safely and had a number of attractive features such as two-speed planetary transmission (making it easy to drive), a detachable cylinder head (making it easy to repair), and a simple four-cylinder, 177-cubic-inch engine producing 22 horsepower at 1600 rpm. The frame and running gear was fashioned from materials that made it lighter and tougher than other cars, while its high chassis was designed to clear the bumps in rural roads. At twenty miles per gallon, it was also economical on fuel.

Ford's marketing approach was simple and universal. It promoted the car using slogans such as these: "It gets you there and it brings you back," "A Ford will take you everywhere except into society," and "Any color you like as long as it is black." There were no annual face-lifts or high-performance models, but there were regular price reductions designed to attract first-time buyers. This was particularly important for U.S. farmers on low incomes who were isolated in remote locations.

The first Model T was priced at $850. With sales on the rise, Ford further slashed the price of the car to make it even more attractive to the mass market. From 1908 to 1913, the price came down from $850 to $600 and sales leaped from 18,000 to 168,000. Meanwhile, the introduction of assembly line production at Ford's factory not only served to bring costs down even further but also slashed the time needed to complete each car from about twelve and a half hours to one and a half. This enabled Ford to meet the rapidly growing demand for Model T. Sales were about 78,000 units in 1911–12 before the assembly line and over 248,000 in 1913–14, after the assembly line was fully in operation. By 1922, Model T sales exceeded a million a year and the price was further cut to $300. Sales peaked at almost 1.8 million in 1923. By that time, more than half the cars on the road were Model Ts. Ford had finally succeeded in putting America on wheels.

However, Ford's success did not last much longer; the company's "one product for all" strategy backfired. The company failed to anticipate that the car that had appealed to the masses could no longer satisfy the changing needs of consumers in an increasingly segmented auto market. By 1927 the General Motors Chevrolet had replaced the Ford Model T as America's number one car. In May of that year, Ford announced the end of production for the Model T even though it was selling at the all-time low price of $290.

The demise of the Model T came about because Ford had failed to see that as the United States urbanized and became richer, consumers began to demand more variety, features, style, and status from their cars. For example, the Model T's lack of speed made it increasingly unattractive to people who valued faster and smoother riding—something that became increasingly important as motorways became more widespread. Similarly, the car's durability and masculinity became a turnoff for women purchasers, a significant and growing segment in the market. Another problem related to financing the Model T's purchase. Banks were reluctant to lend money for car purchases and Ford's refusal to introduce installment buying alienated a significant market segment, the young car buyers who had low current income but high expected future income.

In short, the market was fragmenting into several distinct consumer segments but Ford insisted on selling all of them the same product. This was a mistake that General Motors, under the brilliant leadership of Alfred Sloan, exploited happily. Not only did Sloan introduce a decentralized organizational structure at GM, he also set upon a strategy to sell different cars for different customer markets at different prices. These cars ranged from the Chevrolet (competing against the Model T at the lower end of the market), to the Pontiac, the Oldsmobile, and the Buick (targeting the middle market), and the Cadillac (at the very top end of the market). So as to avoid internal competition, each GM division and each car model were assigned a specific price range and clear customer segments to aim for. General Motors also started a revolution in car styling. It employed the industry's first stylist, Harley Earl, who shaped cars according to taste and fashion rather than functionality. He also created the notion of "model year" by face-lifting cars every year. As with fashion wear, this practice encouraged the public to change cars frequently.

GM also introduced several other innovations—the used car trade-in idea, the closed body format, and GMAC (General Motors Acceptance Corporation) to provide loans to buyers of GM cars. The combination of all these tactics led to plummeting sales for Model T and its withdrawal from the market in 1927. Ford tried to fight back against the onslaught of GM by launching the Model A in December 1927. This was an improved version of the Model T, still simple and reliable but larger, sleeker, and more luxurious, coming in a variety of colors. Although it sold relatively well, it did not fight off the competition from GM's Chevrolet. Ford was totally unprepared to change models so the turnover from Model T to Model A was a tortuous, lengthy, and expensive process. Chevrolet responded via the introduction of a new 6-cylinder engine, thus preserving its sales lead over Ford. The Model A was discontinued in 1931 and Ford fell permanently behind GM in car sales.

The Need for Difficult Choices

The Model T example highlights how difficult it is for a company that successfully scales up a market using a certain strategy to abandon that strategy when the market consolidates. Yet that's exactly what needs to happen. Making difficult choices and deciding what customers not to serve and what product features not to emphasize is what strategy is all about. As the market matures and as competition intensifies, it is these choices that allow a firm to differentiate itself relative to competitors.

Choosing a unique position does not mean that the company will face no competition. Nor does it mean that it should not continuously strive to improve its quality or cut its costs. For example, Dell has staked out a unique position in the PC business. So has Enterprise Rent-A-Car in the car rental business, Edward Jones in the brokerage business, and Southwest in the airline business. These unique positions, however, have not made Dell immune from competition from IBM and HP, or Enterprise from Hertz and Avis, or Edward Jones from Merrill Lynch and Smith Barney, or Southwest from Delta and American. Unique positions do not isolate a company from competition. This implies that a company must continuously strive to improve its customer offering (through better value-for-money propositions)—otherwise its competitors will make its unique position unattractive and so steal its customers.

In addition to striving to make its position better, a company must also try to protect its unique strategic position from imitators. But protection does not come from barriers to entry or government legislation. Rather, a strategic position is protected by two things:

- *All the operational activities that a company puts together to perform well in its position.* All these activities must be put together so that they support and reinforce each other. By building a mosaic of self-reinforcing activities, a firm makes it difficult for other competitors to imitate its position because to do so would require them to replicate this elaborate mosaic of activities.

- *The underlying organizational environment—the culture, incentives, and processes that the firm has put together to support and promote its strategy.* For a competitor to imitate a strategic position, it also needs to imitate the underlying environment of the companies occupying that strategic position. This means that by building a tightly knit environment supporting its strategy, a firm makes it difficult for other competitors to imitate it.

From Product to Process and Then Strategic Innovation

In the early prehistory of new markets, competition takes place primarily between different product designs. When a supply-push innovation process creates a new market on the basis of a new technology rather than articulated consumer needs, there is plenty of scope for a wide variety of firms to bring different product designs to market. As we showed in Chapter Three, this is exactly what they do. The survival and success of firms at this stage depends on the viability of their design and their ability to replace it with a new design should the first one fail to gain market acceptance.

However, when a dominant design is established in the market, the basis of competition shifts. Competition between designs is no longer an issue and is replaced by attempts to differentiate what is basically a standard product. Products sharing the same architecture can still appear different if they have different peripheral characteristics. For example, they can be sold in different types of packaging with different names and supported by different images that consumers might identify with. Thus competition between designs is, at least to some extent, replaced by attempts to differentiate different versions of what is basically the same design.

Above all, however, competition after the emergence of a dominant design comes to focus more and more on price. In part, especially in the very short run, price matters because it is in the overwhelming common interest of all producers to expand the market, and one of the best ways to attract the attention of wavering would-be consumers and propel them into the market is to reduce their acquisition costs. However, a deeper and more long-term process of learning on the demand side of the market reinforces these short-term tendencies to focus on price.

When a product is new and exciting and promises all kinds of unusual benefits, consumers tend to find acquisition costs relatively unimportant compared to their desire to get their hands on this wonderful new product. However, when that product comes to be taken for granted and when differences in peripheral characteristics are perceived to be no more than just minor variations, then value-for-money considerations turn the focus toward minimizing costs. Thus, with the emergence of a dominant design, consumers' preferences gradually become better and better articulated. What this means is that consumers come to value the new good with some precision and compare the merits of spending money on it with those of the other purchasing options they face. Naturally, this makes them more price-conscious.

As the basis of competition comes to focus more and more on price, the sources of competitive advantage lie increasingly with lowering costs. As noted, the choice of a dominant design often sparks a race down learning curves, triggering large investments in plant and equipment that help firms exploit economies of scale. These investments reduce costs and facilitate the fall in prices that, in turn, helps to expand the market during its rapid growth phase. The stronger the competition that firms face and the weaker the opportunities to differentiate their products from rival offerings, the more likely they are to aggressively seek out further opportunities to cut costs. This, in turn, is likely to hasten the shakeout that follows the emergence of the dominant design and force the pace of industry consolidation. Both these tendencies will drive up levels of market concentration, leaving sales in the hands of the top three or four producers in the market. Thus the shift to price competition is likely to lead to major structural changes on the supply side, consolidating the hold that early first movers have on the market.

However, this need to reduce costs can also trigger other changes that also have profound longer-term consequences. The first of these changes is a shift away from product competition toward process competition.

A Shift to Process Competition

When a dominant design becomes established in a market, it brings to an end a period when different designs compete with one another for a place. Although some scope for new product innovation remains, such opportunities center largely around either creating new products to serve very particular niches or adding new peripheral characteristics to the existing dominant design.

As a consequence, it is always going to seem likely that much of the most interesting product innovation activity in a market happens before the emergence of a dominant design. Much of what happens after is inevitably going to seem like small potatoes. What is more, the increasing emphasis on reducing prices and therefore on reducing costs creates strong incentives for firms to invest in process innovations. Anything that reduces costs appreciably is likely to improve a firm's competitive position and will do so with much more certainty than a new product innovation.

Hence the emergence of a dominant design is likely to signal a shift in innovative activity away from product innovation toward process innovation.

When this happens, it can have several interesting consequences much later down the line when the new market has been established for many years. Since process innovation is much harder to spot than product innovation, the shift toward process innovation is going to make the now mature market look technologically stagnant. Consumers will become totally used to what is, after all, a relatively unchanging product and will come to regard it as a commodity. Since price is what drives the purchase of commodities, this gradual change in consumer attitude will reinforce the incentives that producers have to lower their costs, driving them further down the path of process innovation at a time when it might be more sensible for them to make investments in developing new product designs. Indeed, long-standing market leaders in mature markets are often very vulnerable to the competitive challenge posed by new entrants who come into the market pioneering new product or business model innovations.

Enter Strategic Innovation

It is at this stage in the market's evolution that business model or *strategic* innovation becomes an important source of competitive advantage. Strategic innovation is simply the discovery of a new business model or an unexploited position in the industry. New business models invade a market by emphasizing different product or service attributes from those emphasized by the traditional business models of the established competitors. Consider, for example, online brokerage: whereas traditional brokers sell their services on the basis of their research and advice to customers, online brokers sell on the back of a different value proposition, namely price and speed of execution. This point is made vividly clear in Table 7.1, which compares and contrasts the performance attributes emphasized by established firms versus those emphasized by innovators in a number of industries.

Table 7.1. Critical Performance Attributes Emphasized by Established and New Business Models.

Industry	Performance Attributes Emphasized by Established Business Models	Performance Attributes Emphasized by New Business Models
Banking	Extensive nationwide branch network and personal service	Twenty-four-hour access, convenience, price
Insurance	Personal, face-to-face advice through an extensive agent network	Convenience and low commission rates
Airlines	Hub-and-spoke system, premium service, meals, baggage checking	Price, no frills
Brokerage	Research and advice	Speed of execution and price
Photocopying	Speed of copying	Price, size, and quality
Watches	Accuracy and functionality	Design
Steel	Quality	Price
Motorcycles	Speed and power	Size and price
Bookstores	Chain of superstores offering pleasing environment and service	Wide selection, speed, price, convenience
Car Rental	Location (airports) and quality of cars	Location (downtown) and price
Computer	Speed, memory capacity, power	Design and user-friendliness

Since innovators emphasize different dimensions of a product or service, their products or services inevitably become attractive to a different customer base from the one that desires what the traditional competitors offer. As a result, the markets that get created around the new competitors tend to be composed of different customers and have different key success factors from those of the established markets.

This, in turn, implies that since the new markets have different key success factors, they also require a different combination of tailored activities on the part of the firm. For example, the value chain as well as the internal processes, structures, and cultures that Amazon needs to put in place to compete successfully in the online distribution of books is demonstrably different from the one that Borders or Barnes & Noble need to compete in the same industry using *their* business model.

Not only are the new activities required different but often they are also incompatible with a company's existing set of activities. This is because of various trade-offs that exist between the two ways of doing business, which lead to conflicts that make it extremely difficult for an established firm to adopt the new business model and be effective. Because of these trade-offs and conflicts, a company that tries to compete in both positions simultaneously may eventually pay a huge cost and degrade the value of its existing activities. In the meantime, the new business models could grow to challenge the domination of existing business models.

This happens in industry after industry: once-formidable companies with seemingly unassailable strategic positions find themselves humbled by relatively unknown companies that base their attacks on creating and exploiting *new* strategic positions in the industry. This suggests that while fighting it out in its current position, a company must also continuously search for new strategic positions. It has to keep challenging the basis of its existing business and the assumptions that govern its current behavior.

Unfortunately, the majority of companies that strategically innovate by identifying and exploiting new positions in an industry tend to be small niche players or new market entrants. It is indeed rare to find a strategic innovator that is also an established industry big player—a fact that hints at the difficulties of risking the sure thing for something uncertain.

Established players are masters at the game of being better than their rivals but find it much harder to cultivate difference. Likewise, although they are good at competing with rivals who play the "better" game, they are often poor at spotting the emergence of new strategic combinations and combating rivals that exploit them. Established players are so busy fortifying themselves against attack from similar rivals that they fail to notice nimble newcomers whose agility makes the old weapons irrelevant.

For example, Xerox had little trouble protecting its position against fierce competitors like IBM and Kodak, yet lost out to Canon, a little-known camera manufacturer from Japan. Caterpillar saw off the challenge of well-known competitors like International Harvester, John Deere, and J.I. Case, yet lost significant ground to another relatively unknown Japanese company, Komatsu. Broadcaster CBS was able to stand up to ABC and NBC, yet was outflanked by a start-up, CNN. Hertz seems to have little trouble slugging it out with huge competitors like Avis and National, yet is losing ground to little-known Enterprise. And American Airlines is able to stand its ground against fierce global competitors such as British Airways and United but seems to have no answers for Southwest Airlines.

In industry after industry, leading companies are becoming better and better at playing the performance improvement game and have little difficulty stymieing competitors who play by the same rules. Yet these same companies find it extremely difficult to even conceive of a different way of playing the game; they are apt to lose out to any competitor that attacks them by playing a different game. It seems that the better they play their chosen game, the harder they find it to conceive of a different one, and the more easily they fall victim to an upstart that attacks them by playing by different rules.

There are many reasons why established companies find it hard to become strategic innovators. Compared to new entrants or niche players, leaders are weighed down by structural and cultural inertia, internal politics, complacency, fear of cannibalizing existing products, fear of destroying existing competences, satisfaction with the status quo, and a general lack of incentive to abandon a certain present for an uncertain future. In addition, since any industry has fewer leaders than potential new entrants, the chance that the innovator will emerge from the ranks of the leaders is unavoidably small.

Despite such obstacles, established companies cannot afford to ignore strategic innovation. Experience shows that dramatic shifts in company fortunes usually take place when a company succeeds not only in playing its game better than its rivals but also in designing and playing a different game from its competitors. Strategic innovation has the potential to take third-rate companies and elevate them to industry leadership, and it can take established industry leaders and destroy them in a short period of time. Even if the established players do not want to strategically innovate (for fear of destroying their existing profitable positions), somebody else will. Established players might as well preempt that opportunity.

The culture that established players must develop is that *strategies are not cast in concrete*. A company needs to remain flexible and ready to adjust its strategy if the feedback from the market is not favorable. More important, a company needs to continuously question the way it operates in its current position *while* still fighting it out in its current position against existing competitors.

Continuously questioning one's accepted strategic position serves two vital purposes: first, it allows a company to identify early enough whether its current position in the business is losing its attractiveness to others (and so decide what to do about it); second and more important, it gives the company the opportunity to explore the emerging terrain and hopefully be the first to discover new and attractive strategic positions. This is no guarantee: questioning one's accepted answers will not automatically lead to new and unexploited goldmines. But even a remote possibility of discovering something new will *never* come up if the questions are never asked.

Vertical Disintegration

The arrival of a dominant design triggers another major change with profound long-term consequences: production in the industry begins to disintegrate vertically. To understand this conjecture, it is necessary to consider how the early entrants in the market actually produce their products. In these very early days, production runs are small and product designs are fluid. As a consequence, most production methods are likely to be craft-based. That is, producers not only assemble the product they bring to market, they also have to make many of its inputs themselves, particularly those specific to the particular design they are championing.

What all this means is that in the early days of the market, production tends toward very high levels of vertical integration. This situation will probably continue for some time even after the dominant design emerges. Even as the leading firms assemble larger-scale production facilities to produce more economically, they still need to ensure that a readily available supply of specialized inputs exists and that the design of these inputs matches any change in the design of the core product. This makes it convenient (and sometimes absolutely necessary) to keep the production of these inputs in-house.

However, in-house production has a large opportunity cost. If in-house demand for a particular input does not exhaust the full range of scale economies available, then an independent operator who specializes in the production of that input and serves several buyers may end up producing the input at a much lower cost than any in-house operator can. Furthermore, by specializing in the production of that input, the independent operator may also develop an expertise that enables it to innovate faster and more radically than an in-house unit might. As a consequence, the difference between what an in-house supplier and what an independent can offer is likely to widen and gradually tilt the balance away from in-house production as the new market grows and develops. Indeed, in some sectors, final product assemblers may actually manufacture nothing—they just assemble modules made by specialists and then simply ship them to retailers.

The vertical disintegration of production in a market has more profound effects than merely reshaping and resizing leading producers. As the market separating the different components that make up the final product becomes more developed, the costs of using that market decrease (and the opportunity costs of not using it rise). This, in turn, encourages further vertical disintegration, meaning that the increasing size of the market supports an increasingly fine division of labor. Furthermore, as production and expertise become increasingly decentralized, it becomes less and less clear who owns the product in question and who controls its future evolution.

All this creates incentives that encourage product and process innovation at the component level. However, as a market builds up around a finer and finer division of labor in producing the core product, the ability of the existing suppliers and producers to come up with new dominant designs weakens. Thus, as with the shift from product to process innovation, an increase in efficiency in production occurs but at the possible cost of flexibility in product design. The result is that the market—and most of the agents who operate in that market—can get locked into the existing dominant design.

Getting Locked In

For the firms that champion what ultimately becomes the dominant design in a particular market, the process of discovering and then benefiting from first-mover advantages carries both an upside and a downside. The upside is the development of competitive advantages vis-à-vis rivals and later entrants who compete in the market; the downside is vulnerability to innovative entrants who might enter the market by introducing a new dominant design. Existing market leaders often lock themselves into the existing market and develop mindsets, processes, and ways of competing appropriate to that market. They therefore find it difficult to change to something radically new. Like aging dinosaurs, they often trudge off to extinction oblivious of the tremendous changes happening around them. What makes all this a particularly moving and interesting tale is that both the upside and the downside share a set of common causes.

Lock-in arises when firms invest in very specific assets so as to outcompete their rivals. For example, firms make investments in specific and very durable equipment that is good for doing one thing—but only one thing—very efficiently. Firms also build up stocks of knowledge and expertise around doing particular things. As their knowledge base gets more specialized, their ability to do different kinds of things weakens. Finally, efficient organizations always adapt their organizational structures and management systems around their core activities. As competition heats up, the incentive to make investments in such specific equipment, knowledge, and systems increases. However, these investments are very difficult to change when change is necessary. The inevitable consequence of this search for efficiency in the short run is lack of flexibility in the long run.

The desire to get close to the customers is another major cause of lock-in. By getting close to its customers, a firm can serve them better. However, if these same customers turn out to be cautious and conservative, then a firm that chooses to serve them well will opt not to disturb them. This means that such a firm will have only weak incentives to innovate. Furthermore, a firm that focuses too much on its current customers may well miss the opportunity to expand the market through an innovation that is of interest only to new customers. Thus getting close to your customers is fine when they are moving forward but can be detrimental to your health if they are standing still or walking backward.

Firms that get locked in for whatever reason are likely to display some rigidity in their operations. They are likely to focus on current activities and may well neglect promising future developments. This is going to be the case particularly when these future activities threaten the current activities and profits of the firm. Economists call this phenomenon *rent displacement* (everyone else calls it *cannibalization*) and use it to explain why market leaders are less likely to innovate than outsiders that have no stake in the current market.

Whatever its actual causes, the process of lock-in is likely to have important consequences. One is *incumbent inertia*, which makes existing market leaders particularly vulnerable to challenges by outsiders, especially those that bring innovations into the market that threaten to displace the existing dominant design. This threat is real only when the existing dominant design becomes poorly suited to consumers' needs or when it does not fully exploit new technological developments. As we argued earlier, this threat is probably at its most real when the market is mature and the products that embody the dominant design have become commodities.

In a sense, the real issue here is basically one of timing. As long as the prevailing dominant design is winning, virtually all the investments and actions that we have described make good sense. They are what a firm needs to do to remain competitive. However, when the dominant design itself begins to slip, actions that make a firm more adept at supplying products using that design do not necessarily improve its competitiveness. Needless to say, the problems involved in disengaging from the old design and moving toward a new one are exacerbated by the success of the former. The more profitable the existing activities, the harder it is to walk away from them and into the wild and very uncertain world of something new. Success breeds success, until it breeds failure.

Final Thoughts

The use of new technologies to develop an existing dominant design—say, by the addition of more peripheral characteristics or by some rearrangement of the architecture involving the same set of core characteristics—is likely to be a sustaining technological change. For the reasons just discussed, it seems clear that market leaders are likely to have every incentive to push such technological advances as far as they can. However, the displacement of one dominant design by another is likely to be the result of the introduction of a disruptive technology, and successful market leaders—the first movers of yesteryear—are much less likely to emerge as the champions of this kind of technological change. It is sometimes argued that leading firms in markets are sluggish dinosaurs that do not innovate, that they take advantage of the greatest blessing of monopoly power—the ability to enjoy a quiet life. The argument that we have just outlined suggests a more nuanced view. Market leaders may well be very active in seeking out and developing new technologies, but they will be selective in their choice of which technologies to pursue; they may well be very innovative, but they are unlikely to be willing to rock the boat.

Chapter Eight

Creating the Markets of the Twenty-First Century

Name a company that does not aspire to create a new market, enriching itself and its shareholders in the process. Identify a CEO who does not dream of being labeled a visionary for leading an organization into virgin territories, discovering in the process exciting new technologies, products, and markets. We all aspire to become a modern-day Christopher Columbus—the pioneer, the inventor, the adventurer that discovers the industries of the future.

This may be a noble ambition, but *for the majority of big, established companies that aspire to create radically new markets*, it is also a futile one. Such companies are unlikely to be the *creators of new-to-the-world* markets. This is not to say that big, established firms will not discover major new technologies or create major new markets. They will. It is only when it comes to *radical* innovation and the markets that this type of innovation creates that the modern corporation runs into difficulties. You don't have to take our word for it—all you have to do is to examine how the radically new markets of the twentieth century were created to predict how those of the twenty-first century will come about. And all the historical evidence points to one fact: radically new markets are almost never created by big, established firms.

The evidence clearly shows that radical technologies are more likely to originate in the market than inside a firm. As we argued in Chapter Two, it's possible to predict a little bit where they will come from by tracking the various technological trajectories that come close to the market. Similarly, you can anticipate who will bring them to the market by tracing the information highways out of the market.

The evidence also shows that the new dominant design is likely to emerge in a disorganized and chaotic way, with lots of candidate designs championed by lots of new entrants, usually appearing in niches of the existing market. These niches are likely to be populated by consumers who are innovators or early adopters of the new technology. After the design of the new product begins to - stabilize, these early consumers will be the ones responsible for starting the bandwagon rolling. Once that wagon begins to roll, we know that it will pick up speed rapidly and that the market will tip from the old dominant design to the new one almost overnight (or so it will seem at the time). Finally, we know that the champions of the old design— the market leaders of today and the first-movers of yesteryear—will be among those who are least willing to see change occur and least willing to participate in the change process.

Why are the big, established firms unlikely to be the creators of radically new markets? In this book, we have proposed two reasons for such a controversial position: first, big, established companies *cannot* create radically new markets; second, such companies *should not want* to create radically new markets.

Big, established companies cannot create radically new markets primarily because these markets are disruptive to them (as well as to consumers). Any firm preoccupied with serving its existing customers will be blindsided by an innovation process that creates new markets that disrupt its current (winning) way of doing business. Furthermore, the fact that they are disruptive means that radically new markets are not created by customer demand. Instead, they are created by a supply-push process that originates from those responsible for developing the new technology that creates the market. Unfortunately for established firms, supply-push innovation processes share certain characteristics that make them difficult to replicate inside the R&D facilities of the modern corporation. We made this point in Chapter Two.

But there is a second reason why big, established firms cannot create radically new markets: they do not have the skills and attitudes necessary for creating such markets. Worse, they cannot simply adopt the necessary skills and mindsets because of conflict with their existing skills and mindsets.

This sounds negative, but as we suggested in Chapter Four, not everything is bad for established firms! They may not be good at *creating* radically new markets but the truth be told, they don't need to! That's because the money is not in creating the new market but in scaling it up into a mass market. And that's exactly the area where established firms have a competitive advantage over younger firms, because they possess the skills of consolidation that younger firms lack. If that's the case, why would any big, established company want to create a radically new and disruptive market? Surely, the advice we should be giving companies is how to scale up and consolidate new markets, not how to create them.

All this led us to propose that established firms should leave the task of creation to the "market"—the zillions of small start-up firms around the world that have the requisite skills and attitudes to succeed at this game. Established firms should, instead, concentrate on what they are good at—which is to consolidate young markets into big mass markets. They could do this by creating a network of feeder firms—of young, entrepreneurial firms that are busy colonizing new niches. Through its business development function, the established company could serve as a venture capitalist to these feeder firms. It may also help them with its own R&D, more to keep close to technological developments than for any other reason. Then, when it is time to consolidate the market, it could build a new mass-market business on the platform that these feeder firms have provided. Since the younger firms do not have the resources, power, marketing, and distribution to scale up their creations, they should—in principle—be happy to subcontract this activity to the bigger firms, subject to a fair division of the spoils.

Learning from Creative Industries

What we are proposing here is for the modern corporation to sub-contract the creation of new radical products to the market and for start-up firms to subcontract the consolidation of these products to big, established firms. This might strike some people as too radical of an idea but it is in fact a business model that is widely accepted in industries where companies live and die on their ability to *continuously* bring creative new products to the market. We are talking about creative industries such as movies, theater, art galleries, and book and music publishing.[1]

Think about it. A major book publisher does not even try to create any of its "new products" (that is, the season's books) internally. It could, of course, attempt to do exactly that! That would involve hiring thousands of employees, giving them each an office and a computer, and asking them to produce new books in return for a fixed salary (and a generous pension). But how silly does that sound? Surely, an organizational structure like that would be the fastest way to destroy creativity and innovation! And yet, that's exactly how the modern corporation is structured. Is it any surprise, then, that the modern corporation is not particularly known for its creativity and innovativeness?

Instead of attempting to do everything internally, a major book publisher goes out in the market, identifies potential product creators (that is, the authors) and signs them up to deliver their product to it. Once the product is created (outside the bureaucracy of the big firm), the author subcontracts the marketing, promotion, and distribution of the creation to the book publisher. Just as it would be silly for the big publisher to attempt to create the new products internally, it is generally a similar act of folly for individual authors to attempt to sell and promote their books on their own. This division of labor builds upon the strengths of each actor and is a solution that maximizes the welfare of everyone involved. Sure, there may be disagreements and problems between publisher and authors but that's what management is there for.

This arrangement appears to be the norm in several other creative industries. For example, how many art galleries do you know that create their own products (paintings) every year? Conversely, how many famous painters do you know who used to be full-time employees of major galleries in the world? The image of a Picasso or van Gogh laboring away in the R&D laboratory of a major gallery, attempting to create their next masterpiece, is so laughable none of us would take it seriously. Yet, this is exactly how we have organized the modern corporation to deliver new radical products.

As a final example, consider the record industry. It would be hard to envision any of the famous singers and stars of the music industry actually working as full-time employees of the big record companies. Indeed, a recent study of the industry has found that there is a very clear division of labor in this market:[2]

> Large and small firms play different roles in the recruitment of performers and promotion of their albums. The large companies' distinctive competence lies in promotion and record distribution on a large—increasingly, international—scale. The small or independent company performs the gate keeping function of recruiting new artists and, particularly, identifies and promotes new styles of music and types of performers. The distinction closely parallels that between contemporary art galleries that focus on identifying and developing artists with promise and those devoted to promoting successful artists.

Some people might object that the division of labor between creators and promoters in creative industries is easy to achieve because the creators of the product are mostly individuals (authors, singers, painters). Therefore, the argument goes, it would be easy to allow them to operate as free agents and simply sign them up whenever they have something to offer. By contrast, the creation of a new radical product often requires that many scientists work together, usually in the same laboratory, building upon the knowledge and expertise of the organization. This requires some coordination and some supervision of the work.

This is a valid concern, but all you have to do is look at the film industry to understand how the division of labor that we are advocating here could be achieved even when many people are involved in the creation of the product and coordination is necessary. In the film business, a new product (that is, a movie) starts with a screenplay that is often written by an independent agent (the writer). The writer then approaches several producers seeking financing. The producers could be independent or may be partly or wholly owned by distribution companies such as Disney, Sony, Time Warner, Fox, and Viacom. Once a producer acquires the rights to the screenplay, it is that individual's job to line up the financing as well as the director and the actors to produce the movie. Once again, these are all independent agents, willing to offer their services on a specific project for a specific fee. It is only when the product is finally created that the big, established firm—the studio—jumps into action. It acquires the rights to distribute the new product and uses its massive marketing power and existing distribution infrastructure to sell, promote, and distribute the movie.

Therefore, to repeat our thesis, in creative industries we see a clear separation between those that create the product and those that promote, distribute, and sell it. Needless to say, the promoters must be knowledgeable about the latest technology and products so that they can make an intelligent assessment of whether a painting or a book or a record is good enough for them to promote. But they do not have to be actively involved in its creation. If this organization of work functions well in creative industries, shouldn't we at least attempt to import it into other industries that aspire to become more creative? In fact, when we compare the basic economic properties of creative industries with the features that characterize new radical markets (see Table 8.1), it becomes obvious that the two types of markets are amazingly similar. Given this basic fact, we would be surprised if the organizational structure that characterizes creative industries cannot be readily imported into any industry that aspires to create new radical markets.

Table 8.1. The Economic Features of Creative Industries.

Basic Economic Properties of Creative Industries	Applicable to New Radical Markets?
• Demand is uncertain: Nobody knows whether consumers will like the creative product until it is launched.	Yes—all new radical products are experience goods.
• Creative workers care about their product: They will produce art for art's sake whether or not consumers want it.	Yes—colonists are enthusiasts and love their technology.
• Creative products require diverse skills, each meeting a minimum level of proficiency.	Yes.
• Creative products are differentiated: An infinite variety of products can be produced.	Partly applicable.
• The inputs in creative products differ in skill and quality and cannot be standardized.	Applicable only for human input.
• The economic profitability of creative activities relies on close temporal coordination of production and prompt realization of revenues.	Not applicable.
• Creative products are durable and royalties to be derived from them are durable as well.	Partly applicable, especially for intellectual property.

Source: Derived from Richard E. Caves, *Creative Industries: Contracts Between Art and Commerce*, Cambridge, Mass.: Harvard University Press, 2000.

Managing Dual Strategies and Organizations

It's one thing to subcontract creation and another thing to manage the organization that emerges out of such an arrangement. At some point in the process, the established firm would have to move in and pick up the radical product that others have created and scale it up into a mass market. At that stage, the issue for the established company becomes: How can I manage my existing mature business while at the same time managing a young and fast-growing venture next to it?

Such a situation might create two possible problems. First, the established organization may be too old and too efficiency-driven to accommodate a youthful, entrepreneurial venture in its existing infrastructure. Second, the new market may be growing at the expense of the existing business or may require the firm to engage in activities and practices that conflict with those in the established mature business. As a result, the managers of the established business might have incentives to constrain or even kill the new business. In response to these problems, several academics have proposed that the best way to manage the new business is by keeping it separate from the existing organization. That way, you prevent the company's existing processes and culture from suffocating the new business while you give the new unit the autonomy to develop its own culture and strategy and grow without interference from the parent company.

Resorting to a separate organizational entity is certainly a viable option and it is one that several companies have used. For example, IBM chose to set up its PC organization in Boca Raton, Florida, away from the established IBM organization and away from corporate interference. However, this solution has a major drawback: by keeping the two businesses separate, the organization fails to exploit synergies between them. Not only could the new business benefit from the resources and knowledge of the established business, the established business itself could benefit from the vitality and experience of the new business.

In fact, rather than adopting an either/or perspective, an established firm may be better off approaching the issue from a contingency perspective. Specifically, two key factors influence how a firm should manage old and new businesses: how serious the conflicts between the two businesses are—because this determines whether a separation strategy would be especially beneficial or not; and how strategically similar the new market is perceived to be to the existing business—because this determines how important the exploitation of synergies between the two will be. When we plot these two dimensions in a matrix (Figure 8.1), we end up with four possible strategies to managing the two different businesses.

Figure 8.1. Four Strategies for Managing Two Different and Conflicting Businesses.

		A	B
Nature of Conflicts Between the Established Business and the New Market	Serious	Separate	Separate at first and then gradually bring inside
	Minor	D Build it inside and then separate	C Keep inside

Low Strategic Relatedness (different markets)	High Strategic Relatedness (similar markets)

Similarity Between the Established Business
and the New Market

Separation is the preferred strategy when the new market is not only strategically different from the existing business but also poses serious trade-offs and conflicts with it. On the other hand, no separation is necessary when the new market is very similar to the existing business and presents few conflicts that need managing. In such a case, embracing the new business through the firm's existing organizational infrastructure is the superior strategy.

An interesting scenario emerges when the new market is strategically similar to the existing business but the two still face serious conflicts. In such a case, it might be better to separate for a period of time and then slowly integrate the two businesses so as to minimize the disruption from the conflicts. Another interesting scenario arises when the new market is fundamentally different from the existing business but the two are not seriously in conflict. In such a case, it might be better to first build the new business inside the organization so as to take advantage of the firm's existing assets and experience (and learn about the dynamics of the new market) before separating it into an independent unit.

Obviously, deciding when to separate and when to keep the new business inside is only part of the solution. The new business still has to be managed efficiently if it is to succeed against the competitors that will inevitably be drawn into the new market. But that is the topic of another book!

Into the Future

Scientists believe that understanding what happened to the universe in the first few moments after the Big Bang is the key to understanding more or less everything else that has happened ever since. The basic premise of this book is that the same argument could be made about new-to-the-world radical markets. In other words, understanding what happens in the first few moments of their creation is the key to understanding much of that will happen in those markets in the next hundred years.

Therefore, our concern has been with what happens in the very early phases of the development of a radically new market. Like the origin of the universe, this is a subject that is interesting in its own right—as noted in Chapters Two and Three, the early evolution of most markets is packed with interesting incidents. But the real reason for exploring this subject was that much of what happens later on in the life of markets can only be fully understood if one understands how the market itself came into being.

Not only do new markets get created and evolve in a remarkably similar fashion but—what is more—it turns out that it is often rather easy to see the same features in the evolution of most markets in both the New Economy and the Old. In fact, what we see happening today in the development of businesses of the so-called New Economy is very similar to what our great grandparents saw as they watched the development of the automobile industry, the emergence of radio and television, and so on. Indeed, these apparently old businesses were actually harbingers of the new economy of their day—the twentieth century. It seems that what is new in the New Economy is a range of products and services and, in some cases, a delivery mechanism. However, the rules of the game—how they appeared and how the markets for these new products and services developed—are basically the same.

It this book, we explored in detail the way new-to-the-world markets get created, how they evolve, and how companies colonize them. Our goal in adopting a historical approach was to get a clear understanding of the first few moments after the Big Bang that created the new radical market and to assess the structural characteristics of early markets. Based on this understanding, we then offered practical advice to companies on how to go about creating or conquering new markets. In the process, we hope to have provided answers to simple but puzzling anomalies such as these:

- Many ideas have been developed to help big, established companies become more innovative and create new markets. Yet very few radically new markets are actually created by big, established companies. Why is that?

- Many influential academics have been advising companies that the way to become more innovative is to break bureaucracy into small units, change cultures into playful ones, make the strategy process democratic, promote revolutionaries, separate new-business development from the main organization, bring capitalism inside, and so on and so forth. Yet very few established companies have actually done any of these things or enjoyed success from doing them. Why not?

- Many competent companies have moved into new markets that were close to their existing technology and expertise (as when Apple moved into the PDA market or IBM into personal computers). Yet their success rate has not been particularly good. Why is that?

Based on our analysis, we offered practical advice on how big established companies ought to approach new-to-the-world markets.

We are aware that a lot of this advice cuts against the grain of much of the thinking of the last few years, which aimed to make established corporations more entrepreneurial by developing the cultures and structures of the younger start-up firms. We are also aware that this advice may not sit well with established orthodoxies on pioneering, creating new markets, the role of internal R&D in the modern corporation, and many more. This book will have served its purpose if it has challenged you to at least question (if not change) some of these orthodoxies.

Notes

Chapter 1

1. Other authors have called these innovations "architectural" (Henderson and Clark, 1990) or "disruptive" (Christensen, 1997).

Chapter 2

1. Engineering firms typically produce capital goods used by other firms in other industries. These users are sometimes large and powerful and often have very specific needs. They typically have the expertise to master new technologies and to understand how they can benefit from them. It is therefore the case that they will frequently design and build prototypes of the capital goods that they want and pass these on to their suppliers. Furthermore, they use their procurement process to help stimulate innovative activities in their supply chains and to help finance them as well. When they have to compete in very competitive markets downstream they have every reason to try to encourage their suppliers to be more innovative.

2. National Research Council, Computer Science and Telecommunications Board, *Funding a Revolution: Government Support for Computing Research*, Washington, D.C.: National Academy Press, 1999.

Chapter 4

1. Ray Kroc and Robert Anderson, *Grinding It Out: The Making of McDonald's*, Chicago: Regnery, 1977, p. 9.
2. This experiment is described in detail in Robert Sutton, "The Weird Rules of Creativity," *Harvard Business Review*, 2001, 79(8), 94–104.
3. T. Burns and G. M. Stalker, *The Management of Innovation*, Oxford, England: Oxford University Press, 1961.
4. J. D. Day, P. Y. Mang, A. Richter, and J. Roberts, "The Innovative Organization: Why New Ventures Need More Than a Room of Their Own," *McKinsey Quarterly*, 2001, 2, 21–31.
5. M. Iansiti, F. W. McFarlan, and G. Westerman, "Leveraging the Incumbent's Advantage," *Sloan Management Review*, 2003, 44(4), 58–64.
6. Christopher Meyer and Rudy Ruggles, "Search Parties," *Harvard Business Review*, August 2002, pp. 14–15.
7. The network strategy that we are proposing here is not without its risks. Established firms need to worry about identifying appropriate network partners, maintaining control over these partners, staying close to the technology that they themselves do not discover or develop, ensuring proprietary access to the technology developed in somebody else's R&D, and managing the relationship with partners whose cultures and mindsets are fundamentally different from those of the established firm.

Chapter 5

1. A start-up firm might legitimately ask: "Why share my discovery with somebody else?" This is a valid concern but it is based on the flawed belief that the start-up firm has the resources, competences, and power to scale up the discovery. As we have shown, most of them don't. The question

that a start-up firm should ask is: "Do I want to keep 100 percent of (say) a $100 million pie or do I want to have 30 percent of a $1 billion pie?"

2. Our thesis here is that consolidators focus on price and quality and this, in turn, attracts the mass-market consumer. In *Will and Vision*, Gerard Tellis and Peter Golder propose that consolidators start out with a vision of the mass market and then focus on delivering the price and quality that would satisfy their target audience. We believe that both scenarios could play out in reality.

Chapter 6

1. Andrew S. Grove, *Only the Paranoid Survive: How to Exploit the Crisis Points That Challenge Every Company and Career,* New York: Currency/Doubleday, 1996, p. 51.

2. There is only one major exception to this generalization: when someone employs a dramatic technological innovation to attack the leader, seven out of ten market leaders lose out—see the fascinating study by James M. Utterback, *Mastering the Dynamics of Innovation*, Boston: Harvard Business School Press, 1994.

Chapter 8

1. We are indebted to professor Richard Caves for this insight. In conversations with us in 1998 and 1999, he alerted us to the striking similarity between what we are proposing (that is, a division of labor between young and established firms) and what he was observing in his study of creative industries. Professor Caves has since published his work in an excellent book: *Creative Industries: Contracts Between Art and Commerce*, Cambridge, Mass.: Harvard University Press, 2000. Credit must also go to Reid McRae Watts, *The Slingshot Syndrome: Why America's Leading Technology Firms*

Fail at Innovation, Lincoln, Nebr.: Writers Club Press, 2001. This book makes the same link between creative industries and the creation of new radical products and provides a detailed discussion on how the modern corporation could structure itself along the lines that one sees in creative industries.

2. Caves, *Creative Industries*, p. 158.

Further Reading

Chapter 1

For a detailed discussion on the difference between creating and scaling up markets, see Geoffrey A. Moore, *Crossing the Chasm*, New York: HarperCollins, 1991; Gerard J. Tellis and Peter N. Golder, *Will and Vision*, New York: McGraw-Hill, 2002; and Steven Schnaars, *Managing Imitation Strategies*, New York: Free Press, 1994.

An excellent description of the different types of innovation can be found in Rebecca M. Henderson and Kim B. Clark, "Architectural Innovation: The Reconfiguration of Existing Product Technologies and the Failure of Established Firms," *Administrative Science Quarterly*, 1990, 35, 9–30; and Mary Tripsas, "Unravelling the Process of Creative Destruction: Complementary Assets and Incumbent Survival in the Typesetter Industry," *Strategic Management Journal*, 18, Special issue, Summer 1997, 119–142. Disruptive innovation is discussed in detail in Clayton Christensen, *The Innovator's Dilemma: When New Technologies Cause Great Firms to Fail*, Boston: Harvard Business School Press, 1997. Strategic innovation is discussed in C. Markides, *All the Right Moves: A Guide to Crafting Breakthrough Strategy*, Boston: Harvard Business School Press, 1999.

Chapter 2

Much of the argument of this chapter is taken from P. Geroski, *The Evolution of New Markets*, Oxford, England: Oxford University

Press, 2003. For a broader and more extensive discussion of the process of technological change, see D. Mowery and N. Rosenberg, *Technology and the Pursuit of Economic Growth*, Cambridge, England: Cambridge University Press, 1989. On bandwagons and the growth of markets, see E. Rogers, *The Diffusion of Process Innovations*, New York: Free Press, 1995. M. Gladwell, *The Tipping Point*, New York: Little, Brown, 2000, is a popular account, while G. Moore, *Crossing the Chasm*, Oxford, England: Capstone Books, 1991, looks at the subject from a marketing perspective. The television story is well told by D. Fisher and M. Fisher in *Tube: The Invention of Television*, Orlando: Harcourt, Brace, 1996. There are many histories of the development of the Internet, including J. Naughton, *A Brief History of the Future*, London: Weidenfield and Nicholson, 1999, and J. Abbate, *Inventing the Internet*, Cambridge, Mass.: MIT Press, 1999.

Chapter 3

J. Utterback, *Mastering the Dynamics of Innovation*, Boston: Harvard Business School Press, 1994, sets out the theory of dominant designs in a readable form. Much of the work on entry into new markets has been done by a group of sociologists called organizational ecologists; for a readable (if not definitive) text, see G. Carroll and M. Hannan, *The Demography of Corporations and Industries*, Princeton, N.J.: Princeton University Press, 2000. The shakeouts that accompany the arrival of a dominant design are discussed by, among others, S. Klepper and K. Simons, "Technological Extinctions of Industrial Firms," *Industrial and Corporate Change*, March 2000, 6(2), 379–460.

For a history of X-rays and the development of the CAT scanner, see B. Holtzmann Kevles, *Naked to the Bone*, Reading, Mass.: Addison-Wesley, 1998. The development of the U.S. car industry has been widely discussed, including in Klepper and Simons, cited earlier. For an interesting discussion of why cars are powered by gasoline and not electricity, see D. Kirsch, *The Electric Car and the*

Burden of History, Newark, N.J.: Rutgers University Press, 2000. Much of the story of Windows can be gleaned from accounts of the famous Microsoft trial, of which K. Auletta, *World War 3.0*, London: Profile Books, 2001, is one of the best and most readable.

Chapter 4

For a broader and more extensive discussion on the different skills needed for colonization and consolidation, see T. Burns and G. M. Stalker, *The Management of Innovation*, Oxford, England: Oxford University Press, 1961; and J. Heskett, "Establishing Strategic Direction: Aligning Elements of Strategy," Harvard Business School Note #9-388-033, 1987. Michael Porter discusses the reasons that give rise to trade-offs in strategy in "What Is Strategy," *Harvard Business Review*, November-December 1996, pp. 61–78. The experience of Lotus is described in detail in Robert Sutton, "The Weird Rules of Creativity," *Harvard Business Review*, 2001, 79(8), 94–104.

A good exploration of the subject of radical cultural change and how established companies can become better innovators is found in Gary Hamel, *Leading the Revolution*, Boston: Harvard Business School Press, 2000. Gary Hamel has also proposed the idea of "bringing Silicon Valley inside" in an article of that title, *Harvard Business Review*, September-October 1999, pp. 70–84. Other works exploring the topic of enhancing corporate entrepreneurship include Constantinos Markides, "Strategic Innovation in Established Companies," *Sloan Management Review*, 1998, 39(3), 31–42; and Richard Nelson, "Capitalism as an Engine of Progress," *Research Policy*, 1990, 19, 193–214.

The challenge of becoming "ambidextrous" is explored in M. L. Tushman and Charles O'Reilly III, "Ambidextrous Organizations: Managing Evolutionary and Revolutionary Change," *California Management Review*, 1996, 38(4), 8–30. The strategy of separation and creating internal ventures is explored in depth in W. Buckland, A. Hatcher, and J. Birkinshaw, *Inventuring: Why Big*

Companies Must Think Small, London: McGraw-Hill Business, 2003; C. M. Christensen, *The Innovator's Dilemma: When New Technologies Cause Great Firms to Fail*, Boston: Harvard Business School Press, 1997; R. Burgelman, and L. Sayles, *Inside Corporate Innovation*, New York: Free Press, 1986; and C. Gilbert and J. Bower, "Disruptive Change: When Trying Harder Is Part of the Problem," *Harvard Business Review*, May 2002, pp. 94–101. For discussions of the weaknesses and drawbacks of internal ventures, see E. B. Roberts, "New Ventures for Corporate Growth," *Harvard Business Review*, 1980, 58(4), 134–142; D. T. Dunn Jr., "The Rise and Fall of Ten Venture Groups," *Business Horizons*, 1977, 20(5), 32–41; and N. Fast, "A Visit to the New Venture Graveyard," *Research Management*, 1979, 22(2), 18–22.

A masterful examination of creative industries can be found in Richard Caves, *Creative Industries: Contracts Between Art and Commerce*, Cambridge, Mass.: Harvard University Press, 2002. For a good summary on how to exploit open innovation, see Henry Chesbrough, *Open Innovation*, Boston: Harvard Business School Press, 2003; and Andrew Hargadon, *How Breakthroughs Happen*, Boston: Harvard Business School Press, 2003.

For excellent discussions on how big, established firms could use alliances with smaller firms to exploit radical innovations, see David Teece, "Capturing Value from Technological Innovation: Integration, Strategic Partnering and Licensing Decisions," *Interfaces*, 1988, 18(3), 46–61; Reid McRae Watts, *The Slingshot Syndrome: How America's Leading Technology Firms Fail at Innovation*, Lincoln, Nebr.: Writers Club Press, 2001; Francisco-Javier Olleros, "Emerging Industries and the Burnout of Pioneers," *Journal of Product Innovation Management*, March 1986, pp. 5–18; James Hlavacek, Brian Dovey, and John Biondo, "Tie Small Business Technology to Marketing Power," *Harvard Business Review*, January-February 1977, pp. 106–116; and Francisco-Javier Olleros and Roderick J. Macdonald, "Strategic Alliances: Managing Complementarity to Capitalize on Emerging Technologies," *Technovation*, 1988, 7, 155–176. The idea of outsourcing innovation is explored in James Brian Quinn, "Outsourcing Innovation: The New Engine of Growth," *Sloan Management Review*, 2000, 41(4), 13–29; and Christopher Meyer and Rudy Ruggles, "Search Parties," *Harvard Business Review*, August 2002, pp. 14–15.

Chapter 5

A book that sets out the so-called dominant design hypothesis in a very readable form is J. Utterback, *Mastering the Dynamics of Innovation*, Boston: Harvard Business School Press, 1994. There is now a fairly large literature on dominant designs; see among others, J. Utterback and F. Suarez, "Dominant Designs and the Survival of Firms," *Strategic Management Journal*, Summer 1995, 16, Special Issue, 415–430; K. Clark, "The Interaction of Design Hierarchies and Market Concepts in Technological Evolution," *Research Policy*, 1985, 14(5), 235–247; and M. Tushman and J. Murmann, "Dominant Designs, Technology Cycles and Organizational Outcomes," in *Research in Organizational Behavior*, Greenwich, Conn.: JAI Press, 1998.

There are many studies of the battles that have been fought to establish dominant designs or standards in particular markets: on U.K. satellite television, see chapter 7 in P. Ghemawat, *Games Businesses Play*, Cambridge, Mass.: MIT Press, 1997; on VHS versus Betamax, see M. Cusumano et al., "Strategic Manoeuvering and Mass Market Dynamics: The Triumph of VHS over Betamax," *Business History Review*, 1992, 66(1), 51–95. The quads story is recounted in S. Postrell, "Competing Networks and Proprietary Standards: The Case of Quadraphonic Sound," *Journal of Industrial Economics*, 1990, 39(2), 169–186. The account on genetically modified food in the United Kingdom is drawn from a case study written by Lisa Thomas, "The Commercialization of Genetically Modified Foods," London Business School, 1999. On baked beans, see N. Koehn, "Henry Heinz and Brand Creation in the Late 19th Century," *Business History Review*, 1999, 73(3), 349–394. On the Palm story, see A. Butter and D. Pogue, *Piloting Palm*, New York: Wiley, 2002.

There are several excellent books on how a firm can scale up markets. See in particular, Geoffrey A. Moore, *Crossing the Chasm*, New York: HarperCollins, 1991; Gerard J. Tellis and Peter N. Golder, *Will and Vision*, New York: McGraw-Hill, 2002; and Steven Schnaars, *Managing Imitation Strategies*, New York: Free Press, 1994.

Chapter 6

For an excellent discussion of second-mover strategies see Steven Schnaars, *Managing Imitation Strategies*, New York: Free Press, 1994. For a summary of the theoretical arguments for first-mover advantages as well as the empirical support for them, see chapter 1 of Gerard J. Tellis and Peter N. Golder, *Will and Vision*, New York: McGraw-Hill, 2002. The strategy of breaking the rules that latecomers could adopt is discussed in C. Markides, "Strategic Innovation," *Sloan Management Review*, 1997, 38(3), 9–23.

Chapter 7

The subjects discussed in this chapter have generated a vast literature, and our coverage of them has necessarily been selective. The issue of rapid growth associated with the scaling up of a market is explored in Geoffrey A. Moore, *Inside the Tornado: Marketing Strategies from Silicon Valley's Cutting Edge*, New York: HarperCollins, 1995. A good discussion on the need to make difficult choices in strategy can be found in C. Markides, *All the Right Moves: A Guide to Crafting Breakthrough Strategy*, Boston: Harvard Business School Press, 1999; and M. Porter, "What Is Strategy?" *Harvard Business Review*, November-December 1996, pp. 61–78. The Who-What-How framework proposed in this chapter was originally developed by Derek Abell, *Defining the Business: The Starting Point of Strategic Planning*, Englewood Cliffs, N.J.: Prentice Hall, 1980.

Interesting work on lock-in and incumbent inertia includes C. Christensen, *The Innovator's Dilemma: When New Technologies*

Cause Great Firms to Fail, Boston: Harvard Business School Press, 1997; and C. Markides, "Strategic Innovation in Established Companies," *Sloan Management Review*, 1998, 39(3), 31–42. The topic of strategic innovation is covered in C. Markides, "Strategic Innovation," *Sloan Management Review*, 1997, 38(3), 9–23.

A nice summary of the literature of first-mover advantages can be found in K. Montgomery and M. Lieberman, "First-Mover Advantages," *Strategic Management Journal*, Summer 1988, 9, Special issue, 41–58; and Venkatesh Shankar, Gregory Carpenter, and Lakshman Krishnamurthi, "Late Mover Advantage: How Innovative Late Entrants Outsell Pioneers," *Journal of Marketing Research*, February 1998, 35, 54–70. The hypothesis on vertical disintegration in markets was first advanced by G. Stigler, "The Division of Labour is Limited by the Extent of the Market," *Journal of Political Economy*, 1951, 59(3), 185–193. The hypothesis on the shift from product to process innovation originated with W. Abernathy and J. Utterback, "Patterns of Industrial Innovation," *Technology Review*, 1978, 80(7), 40–47. See also J. Utterback, *Mastering the Dynamics of Innovation*, Boston: Harvard Business School Press, 1994.

Acknowledgments

This book has been far too long in the making. Its thesis was originally conceived about six years ago when we co-taught an MBA course at London Business School titled Market Change and Strategy. The thesis has since undergone numerous transformations, rethinking, and (to put it politely) pauses for reflection. We gratefully acknowledge the feedback and comments of our colleagues Yiorgos Mylonadis, Freek Vermeulen, and Phanish Puranam, and we thank the numerous executive and MBA students who have been subjected to lectures and debates on the issues raised in the book. A special thank you also to Angelos, Maria, and Yiorgos, who provided critical comments on earlier drafts.

During this long gestation period, we have both been pursuing projects that have ended up having quite a big impact on the book's content. Much of Geroski's work culminated in *The Early Evolution of Markets*, published by Oxford University Press in 2003. Markides has spent much of these years looking at the whole process of strategic innovation. This work has culminated in several published articles and is now providing the raw material for his new (and forthcoming) book, *Strategic Innovation: The Incumbent's Response*.

Every May, we both spent time in Crete teaching at the Mediterranean Agronomic Institute of Chania. The original plan was to spend part of that time writing this book. However, the generous hospitality of the Institute's director, Alkis Nicolaides, plus the never-ending distractions provided by Alice, Rosa, and Andreas, succeeded in ensuring that Crete was the one place where no useful work on the book was actually done! We have no regrets for this, and indeed, we would like to dedicate the book to Alkis, Alice, Rosa, and Andreas by way of thanks for making sure that our sojourns in Crete were, to say the least, memorably unproductive.

August 2004   P.A.G.
                                                     C.C.M.

The Authors

CONSTANTINOS C. MARKIDES is professor of strategic and international management and holds the Robert P. Bauman Chair of Strategic Leadership at the London Business School. A native of Cyprus, he received his BA (Distinction) and MA in economics from Boston University, and his MBA and DBA from the Harvard Business School. He has worked as an associate with the Cyprus Development Bank and as a research associate at the Harvard Business School.

He has done research and published on the topics of strategic innovation, corporate restructuring, refocusing, and international acquisitions. His *Diversification, Refocusing and Economic Performance* was published by MIT Press in December 1995, and *All the Right Moves: A Guide to Crafting Breakthrough Strategy* was published by Harvard Business School Press in November 1999. A third book, coedited with Michael Cusumano of MIT and titled *Strategic Thinking for the Next Economy*, was published by Jossey-Bass in May 2001.

His publications have also appeared in journals such as the *Harvard Business Review, Sloan Management Review, Directors & Boards, Leader to Leader, Long Range Planning, Business Strategy Review, British Journal of Management, Journal of International Business Studies, Strategic Management Journal*, and the *Academy of Management Journal*.

He has taught on many in-company programs and is on the Academic Board of the Cyprus International Institute of Management. He is also a non-executive director of Amathus

(UK) Ltd, a tour-operating company. He is associate editor of the *European Management Journal* and is on the Editorial Board of the *Strategic Management Journal* and the *Sloan Management Review*. He is a member of the Academy of Management and the Strategic Management Society and a Fellow of the World Economic Forum in Davos, Switzerland. His current research interests include the management of diversified firms and the use of innovation and creativity to achieve strategic breakthroughs. You can reach him by e-mail at cmarkides@london.edu.

PAUL A. GEROSKI is chairman of the Competition Commission and a member of the economics subject area at London Business School (where he is a professor of economics). His current research interests are focused on innovation, technological change, and the evolution of markets, and on regulation and competition policy. His books include *Market Dynamics and Entry* (Basil Blackwell, 1991); *Innovation, Market Structure and Corporate Performance* (Oxford University Press, 1994); *Coping with the Recession* (with Paul Gregg, Cambridge University Press, 1997); and *The Early Evolution of New Markets* (Oxford University Press, 2003), as well as numerous articles on corporate performance, innovation, business strategy, and industrial and antitrust policy.

He has sat on the editorial boards of several journals (and has served on the boards of several others), on the Council of the Royal Economic Society, and on the board of Greater London Enterprises Ltd. and Graseby plc. He served as president of the European Association for Research in Industrial Economics (EARIE) from 1995 to 1997 and the Industrial Organization Society in 1997, and was a governor of London Business School. He is currently a research fellow at the Centre for Economic Policy Research (CEPR). You can reach him by e-mail at pgeroski@london.edu.

Index